ANSWERING
THE CRY

by Kenneth Eagle
as told to Virginia Crider

CHRISTIAN LIGHT PUBLICATIONS, INC.
Harrisonburg, Virginia 22801-1212

Christian Light Publications, Inc.
Harrisonburg, Virginia 22801-1212
© 1976 by Christian Light Publications, Inc.
All rights reserved. Published 1976
Printed in the United States of America

06 05 04 03 02 01 00 99 98 97   5 4 3 2

Cover by Martha Yoder

ISBN 0-87813-510-3

TABLE OF CONTENTS

PREFACE

This book is a sequel to *Cry of the Northland.* While it follows the story begun in that book, it does not depend upon its predecessor for clarity, interest, or understanding.

Names of most places are fictitious. A few, such as Red Lake, York Factory, and Big Trout Lake, have been allowed to stand.

All main characters are real persons with the exception of Jay Meekis, who is a composite of numerous elements. Not all events are recorded precisely as they happened. To simplify the narrative, many details concerning the development of Bear River School have been omitted. While the marriage of Jimmie Byler and Lydia Brooks took everyone by surprise, Kenneth Eagle probably knew of it before arriving at Bear River, as the book relates it. Joe Brooks was not married at the time he appears on the scene, contrary to what the story relates. Other discrepancies such as these are possible.

Brother Eagle also states that many years passed before he learned the full story of Curly's move to Red Lake. As the book relates the account, Brother Eagle kept abreast of these developments through other persons.

My thanks go to Northern Light Gospel Mission personnel for the generous assistance they have given in acquiring the material necessary for this book. I also want to thank those who have given freely of their time in reading the manuscript and in offering suggestions for its improvement. I appreciate also the services of Margaret Thompson and Annie Quill, who acted as interpreters for me during my last visit to Red Lake.

The author wishes to acknowledge the contribution of many persons to the spreading of the Gospel in the North, whose names do not appear in these pages, mainly because she has lacked opportunity to meet them and hear their stories. The fact that they are not included in this account does not make them any less a part of the Lord's answer to the cry of the Northland.

March 5, 1975   B.V.C

I

CRY OF THE NORTHLAND

The clock on the mantel of our Rockydale, Pennsylvania, home struck 11 p.m. My worn suitcase stood by the door, packed, ready for my departure in the morning. That valise had accompanied me during many miles of travel, including many states in the South as well as the northern bush country. Strangely, as I think of it now, I had no premonition of the importance of this upcoming Virginia revival to bringing the message of salvation in Christ to the people of the Northland.

My wife Susie eyed me critically.

"That suit really needs pressing, Dear," she lamented.

I surveyed the limp creases in the legs of my trousers. They certainly would profit from the application of a hot iron.

"Take the suit off and I'll press it for you when I've finished these dishes," Susie suggested, picking up a stack of plates and placing them in the sudsy pan.

I looked at the pile of dishes still to be done. "No, Dear," I objected. "I'll do the suit myself. You have enough to do yet with all those dishes. I've done it before, you know," I said reassuringly.

I donned a worn pair of trousers from an old suit, set up the ironing board, and hooked up the iron.

I brushed the garment thoroughly while the iron heated. Several stubborn spots on the cuffs demanded special care and the iron heated more than I had anticipated. When I placed the appliance on the garment, an odor akin to singed feathers filled the room.

"Oh, no!" I groaned, lifting the iron to view the damage.

"Didn't you use a damp cloth, Kenneth?" Susie inquired, turning away from the sink to investigate.

"I completely forgot," I mourned.

We studied that burned spot. "What will I do, Susie?

I can't wear it like that," I declared. "That spot is right on the knee, where everyone can see it."

"And it is your only good suit," Susie answered thoughtfully. She stood a moment, her hand immersed in suds. "I guess you'll have to borrow a suit, Dear."

"Borrow a suit!" I cried. "But . . ."

"What else can you do?" Susie insisted. "You can't wear this one; you don't have another one, and . . ."

"Yes, yes, I see," I nodded. I set my mind to work, considering possibilities for finding a suit the right size that I might be able to borrow.

"Say!" I exclaimed after searching through a gallery of friends and relatives for someone nearly my size, "I believe Art Good is about my build. Why don't I try him?"

"My cousin?" Susie replied. "The man who filled your scooter tank when you ran out of gas one Sunday?" She smiled happily. "Didn't he tell you that day to come to him if you needed assistance in the Lord's work?"

"Yes," I replied, but added ruefully, "I'm sure he didn't expect it to be a request to borrow his good suit!"

However, if Art thought my request strange when I called him, he certainly didn't let on. And his suit, while not a perfect fit, did pass the critical inspection of Mrs. Good and Susie.

"May the Lord bless you, Art," I said, gripping his hand firmly as we parted.

Art chuckled. "I'm so happy you thought of me, Kenneth. If you ever need anything else, please call us."

Praising God for Christian brothers, Susie and I placed the suit in our car and drove back to the hills.

Early on Saturday morning Susie bundled the children into their winter wraps and drove me to the depot. We chatted cheerfully of Christmas, which loomed just weeks away. Too soon we drew up before the station.

I bade the children good-bye, then Susie. Teasingly, I asked, "Are you going to cry after I'm gone, Susie?"

She smiled. "Probably."

I'm not ashamed to confess that tears dampened my eyes as the train once again carried me away from my loved ones: Susie; blond, blue-eyed Michael; black-eyed, raven-haired Joyce; and baby Luke, who at four years of age hardly seemed like a baby.

As the miles zipped by beneath me, I recalled a letter from Allen Martz that had arrived only yesterday. My friend of many years was engaged in spreading the message of God's love in the outlying areas of northwestern Ontario. Due to the crush of preparations, I had scanned it only briefly. Now I settled back to read the letter more carefully.

The postmark, I noticed, bore the Loman, Minnesota, stamp. Evidently Allen had mailed it while spending the weekend with Betsy and the children. I began reading.

"In spite of some problems," Allen began after greeting me, "we have much to be thankful for. The people at Marshy Lake have learned that we have a nurse, Mamie Black, stationed at Bear River. They would like to see a similar operation at Marshy Lake. We are looking for a couple to live at Marshy in addition to a nurse. Mamie Black, along with Jimmie Byler and Lydia, are at Bear River. You remember Jimmie, don't you?" I realized much later that I had completely overlooked that phrase, "Jimmie Byler and Lydia." Its significance didn't strike me at all.

I almost laughed outright at Allen's question, "You do remember Jimmie, don't you?" Did I remember Jimmie? How could I forget him?

A vivid recollection of my visit with Jimmie at Bear River flashed through my mind. Again I recalled those breathless moments when Jimmie had told me of the forced landing he and Allen had made in the small mission plane. The craft had come down in a northern lake and had sunk. Neither man could swim. Listening to Jimmie relate the incident had been an unforgettable experience.*

Brushing aside those memories, I read, "Within the last few weeks we have had four deaths at the bush stations—four funerals and four souls in eternity. We wonder, 'Who will be next? Will they be ready to meet the Lord?' This may very well depend upon us. We, of this generation, are the only ones who can bring the

Gospel to our generation. We are responsible."

The letter dropped from my hand. Again I heard the voice of the Indian brother at Bear River. "Why did you wait so long to come? Why did you wait so long to tell us?" I heard other voices begging us to send people to tell them about God and how they can be saved through faith in Jesus.

My burden grew as I read the last paragraph of Allen Martz' letter. "Our problem at the present is that people want to give six weeks to two years of service but do not consider giving their lives. This does not give them a genuine desire to fit into the work or to make an effort to learn the Indian language. They often do well in hard physical labor, but we sense a lack of concern for the salvation of souls."

My heart ached. I cried out to the Lord for the lost souls of the Northland. And, unknown to me, the Lord would use me in answering that cry. He moves in strange ways.

Although I had never conducted a series of meetings since that memorable trip north without speaking of the Indian people and their longing for the Gospel, I had no reason to connect these current meetings in Virginia with Allen Martz or the Gospel outreach at Red Lake.

Not even after meeting Clayton Drake.

It came about in this way. One evening following the revival service, a knock sounded at the door of the home of my minister host. A young man asked to speak with me. He introduced himself as Clayton Drake, a junior student at our nearby church college.

"Your name sounds like a nice, fat duck," I quipped, gripping his hand heartily.

"Yours isn't exactly complimentary itself," he shot back, grinning.

We sat down, immediately at ease with each other. "Clayton, why did you wish to see me? What is your problem?" Something about the youth appealed greatly to me. I couldn't put my finger on it, but I longed to help him, whatever his difficulty.

Clayton didn't waste words. "Brother Eagle, how can I find God's will for my life?" he asked.

I studied a moment. "Clayton," I stated

emphatically, "I think conviction is the most important thing in finding God's will for us. What is your conviction? What do you believe the Lord *wants* you to do?"

Slowly, sitting forward in his chair, clasped hands propped on his knees, Clayton replied, "I've always felt that I would like to teach among an aboriginal people, perhaps in Brazil," he stated hesitantly. "But you see," he added, "whenever I think of going there, a wall seems to be standing between me and them, as if this is not the Lord's will for me."

To this day I can't explain what prompted me to say—except, of course, that God directed me by His Spirit—"Clayton, in two weeks I'll be holding meetings in Montana. From there I'll be going to Red Lake, Ontario. The Lord is using Allen Martz to carry the message of salvation in Christ into many of the areas surrounding Red Lake. People have responded to the Gospel. Allen wants me to visit some of these brethren and encourage them in their faith. It will be during your Christmas holidays."

I studied Clayton seriously. Would he accept the suggestion I was about to make? I could only offer it and see. "Why don't you ask for an extended leave from school and meet me in Minnesota on December . . . let's see . . ." I glanced at my pocket calendar. "Why don't you meet me on December 28 at International Falls, Minnesota, and I'll take you north with me. Perhaps the Lord will speak to you through that experience."

Clayton agreed readily to the proposal. We worked out the details for meeting at International Falls on December 28, 1958.

As Clayton departed, I wondered, "Will I ever see Clayton Drake again? What are the Lord's plans for this extremely personable and talented young man? And why had the Lord chosen to cross his path with mine—or mine with his?"

I should have recognized by this time that God does nothing haphazardly or without design!

*See *Cry of the Northland*.

II

THAT MATTER OF MONEY . . .

As I prepared for the trip to Montana, other considerations forced Clayton Drake from my mind.

"I need grocery money, Dear," Susie said as she carefully packed my white shirts in the suitcase. With a twinge of nostalgia, I remembered how the Lord had spoken to Susie and me through those white shirts some years before. How very literally the Lord had fulfilled His word!

"I know, Susie," I returned, "but I have just enough money for train fare out to Montana. I'll send you some grocery money from there." I was depending upon the offering from the congregation to supply our need since the Lord had used this method many times previously in easing our financial straits.

"All right," Susie agreed, closing the hasp on the battered bag. "We can get by that long."

Some years before, Susie and I had covenanted together to give full time to the Lord's work. In return, we promised to trust Him to supply our physical necessities. Thus far the Lord had proved faithful, although I must confess that at times our faith had been weak. We had been inclined to doubt His care of us. Now another time of testing stared us in the face although we were not aware of it at that moment.

Train rides provide ample time for correspondence. As the locomotive sped westward, I took a neglected letter from Jimmie Byler out of my coat pocket.

Jimmie wrote, after the usual warm greetings, "I accompanied Peter King and his brother Sam on their trap lines last week. Working together in this way offers many opportunities to share the good things of the Lord. I offered (almost to my sorrow!) to carry some of their catch for them. Carrying a dead fox or beaver several miles on snowshoes is work!"

I visualized Jimmie's flashing smile as he uttered those statements. I pictured his slight figure, with a fox draped over his shoulder or a beaver pelt hanging down his back, trudging across the snow. I had disposed of enough carcasses during my farming days to know something of the weight of dead animals.

Jimmie continued, "While working the trap line with Peter, I became ill due to drinking water that was too cold. When Sam learned of my distress, he brewed herb tea for me. I felt better immediately."

My mind reverted to the days of my youth when Mother would go outdoors and gather plants to be used in dealing with different illnesses. Some cures, such as mint tea, were delicious. Others we would gladly have done without!

"Do you remember Jay Meekis?" Jimmy inquired. Yes, I recalled the tall man who had brought a motor to Jimmie for repairs during my visit to Bear River. For some reason he and Jimmie did not "hit it off," and this concerned my friend terribly. "His attitude seemed to have changed (or more likely, mine did!), and he invited us to have services in his home. Recently we discovered that through some misunderstanding he expected us to pay rent for the use of his dwelling."

"While we puzzled over the matter," Jimmie wrote, "a note written in English arrived, inviting us to have services in another home. This seemed to be the Lord's answer to our dilemma. We arrived there to find 100 people waiting for us. Surely God is good."

The outskirts of Chicago rushed by as I pondered the matter. God had been good, yes. But what of Jay Meekis? Would he accept this rebuff kindly? Or would he consider it a personal insult?

I found Jimmie shared my fears. "I'm afraid Jay may not take too kindly to this arrangement," he surmised. "I wonder if we acted wisely. We did what appeared to be the Lord's will at the time." (Although I did not know it at this time, when this situation came up again, they did pay rent for the use of a dwelling.)

His letter ran on. "Lest you decide we have no victories, let me report what the Lord has done. Recently a Christian brother stopped by, asking me to come to his home. His unsaved wife was very ill. He asked me, according to Mark 16, to lay hands on her and pray for her recovery. I don't hesitate, Brother Eagle, to say that I experienced quite a struggle before I was ready to step out in faith and agree to his request."

I nodded in silent understanding. I recalled distinctly my own fierce trial before I, too, claimed God's promise for healing in the behalf of our Joyce.* Eagerly I perused the letter further. What had happened? I must know.

"I spoke to Sarah," Jimmie related, "asking her if she believed the Lord could heal her and if she desired Him to do so. She replied with a firm yes to both questions. We laid hands upon her and prayed in the name of Jesus."

I couldn't wait to find out how the incident had ended. "The next morning John stopped by to say that his wife was no longer ill. He added that she was no longer a follower of her old religion, since it had not helped her. 'Maybe she'll soon be a Christian, like we are,' he added."

I sensed Jimmie's great joy with this victory. But more followed.

"In another home, the mother Beulah was very ill. Her son Joel attends Sunday school regularly. He 'put out a fleece' as Gideon did, by placing his New Testament on the bed beside his mother. He prayed, 'Lord, if the stories I have heard in Sunday school about how You heal people are true, then make my mother well.' Beulah recovered, and Joel gave his heart to the Lord."

My own heart overflowed.

"Another joy," Jimmie stated, "is the concern of believers for their unsaved neighbors and friends. When they return from the trap line, they immediately want to know if anyone has come to the Lord during their absence. They spend hours studying the Word and go to great lengths to bring others in."

"If only our brethren were so enthusiastic," I mused.

"One of our greatest hindrances is the other local missionary who preaches an easy Christianity. Another drawback is the white trader who is fair and honest, but unsaved," Jimmy explained. "The people consider the trader a Christian because he is honest. They cannot see the need for an inner change. Both men cause untold problems."

I could imagine. The missionary would not like to be proved wrong, nor would the trader want to be shown that he was a sinner in God's sight. Yet both were necessary if the people were to be converted.

Jimmie concluded, "While the Gospel found its way to Bear River many years ago, and most persons have some knowledge of the Bible, we find few individuals who have experienced the new birth. Those who do know Christ have real joy and peace in their hearts. It is our desire that many more who are bound by Satan and his devices will come to know the salvation Christ brings."

Without even glancing at the signature—Jimmie and Lydia Byler—I replaced the letter in the envelope.

More people *must* be found who would be willing to work in this part of God's vineyard. I prayed earnestly that God would send laborers into this field.

I arrived in Montana to find a small congregation of very poor people. This in itself did not bother me. In fact, I like this type of ministry. The only hitch came when the deacon handed me the offering. Somehow I had failed to anticipate so small a check.

Discouraged, I thought of Susie. I had promised to send grocery money. But I also needed train fare east to Minnesota. Money to return home from Red Lake had to come from some place. This amount would not begin to cover traveling expenses. Discouraged, I felt my Lord had failed me, that He had let me down.

Brother Lewis, the deacon, suggested, "Let me take you out to the prairie to catch the train, Brother Eagle. That will save some train fare for you."

That was fine with me. I literally "caught" the train with one hand while grasping my suitcase with the other. I stumbled to a seat.

My black mood deepened. We passed through Devil's Lake, North Dakota. "How appropriate! That's just how I feel," I muttered beneath my breath. "This must be Devil's County. I wonder what place comes next?"

Finally we pulled into Grand Forks, North Dakota. Here I had to change trains. I could not know that it would also prove to be the "grand forks" in my trip—that decisive events here would break the bonds of discouragement which gripped me.

Truly His ways are "past finding out."

*See *Cry of the Northland*.

III

THE BLESSING OF THE LORD

The memory of my mother's deathbed blessing was the farthest thing from my mind when I alighted from the train at Grand Forks that blustery winter day. In fact, had it occurred to me at that moment, I would probably have disdained it in preference for cold, hard cash! However, I do believe the events of that day took place partly as a result of Mother's prayer.

In checking with the station master, I discovered a layover of five hours in Grand Forks. As I sat waiting, I became very hungry.

"No," I scolded myself, "you can't have anything to eat. Your money won't last as it is."

My stomach didn't heed the rebuke. It continued rumbling. "Ten cents won't make that much difference," I decided. "I'll go out and get a bowl of soup."

I walked out of the station and located a restaurant. I started walking toward it.

A man tottered toward me. He placed a trembling hand on my arm. "Eh-h-h, Brother, can you spare a dime for a bowl of soup?" he quavered.

I struggled with my emotions. I could say, "If you didn't drink up all your money, you wouldn't need a dime," but that wouldn't be right.

Another choice popped into my mind. I might say truthfully, "I can't spare a dime." Yet, reason prompted, I had planned on spending just that amount on myself so obviously I *could* spare it. The matter boiled down to whether I would use the dime upon myself or for this poor alcoholic wretch before me. However, I found one loophole, so I tried squeezing through it.

"I'm sorry," I began, "but I can't give you any money. If I did, you'd drink it right up."

Pathetically the man pleaded, "Oh, no, Sir. I haven't eaten for three days. I need something to eat. Just give me a dime for a bowl of soup, Sir."

I thought of my own empty stomach and my scant resources and the bowl of soup I had planned to get. I studied the derelict man who watched me hopefully. Indecision racked my mind. If I fed him, I would probably have to give up my own meal. What would Jesus do?

"Well," I stated after considering that question, "if you'll go along with me to the restaurant, I'll pay for your meal."

We took seats at the counter. "Could I have a hamburger?" my guest asked.

"Hey," I thought rebelliously, "you asked for a bowl of soup!" But I had agreed to pay for his lunch, so I had little choice but to agree.

"Yes, you may," I nodded, conscious that already my pocketbook would be minus more than the dime originally requested.

My friend gulped that hamburger like a hungry hound. He turned to me again. "Now may I have a bowl of soup?"

"Yes, you may," I consented. "My money won't reach anyway," I thought bitterly, "so what difference does it make?"

"Are you a Father?" my companion turned to ask abruptly as he wolfed the soup.

"Yes, I am a father."

"I thought so!" he declared triumphantly.

"I'm the father of three children," I clarified.

"Oh, I didn't mean a father in that way," he objected. "I mean, are you a priest?"

"No, I'm not a Catholic," I replied.

My companion drained the soup bowl. "May I have a cup of coffee now?" he wondered.

"Wait a minute!" I braked mentally. "You asked for a dime!" But I remembered in time that Jesus would probably have spent His *last* dime in feeding this man. So I said, "Yes, you may."

"Well," the fellow demanded as he sipped his coffee, "if you aren't a Father, who are you anyway?"

Uneasily I noticed that most of the people occupying tables in the restaurant were eavesdropping on our conversation. Indeed, they could not do otherwise, since my "friend" repeated and amplified everything I said. Among the group sat several men clad in long, heavy coats and huge fur caps of the type worn by some Russian people. They presented a formidable appearance.

"I'm a Christian," I told him quietly, hoping that my muted reply would inspire a similar reaction in him.

He mulled over that as he drained the coffee cup. Placing the empty cup on the counter, he patted his stomach experimentally and remarked, "I'm still hungry. Could I have a repeat order?"

"There goes my bowl of soup!" I wailed inwardly, mentally totaling the bill. However, since I had bargained to pay for the meal, I might just as well go all the way. I agreed to the repeat order.

"You say you're a Christian," the man remarked as he dug into the second bowl of soup. "What church do you belong to?"

In a tiny voice I answered, "I'm a Mennonite."

"A Mennonite!" he shouted. Everyone in the building must have heard him. They all stared at me.

One of the men wearing a fur cap left his table and walked over to me. I shook in my shoes.

"Oh," I shivered fearfully, "he heard this man say that I'm a Mennonite. He's probably a warmonger and one of those fellows who hates conscientious objectors. He knows I'm nonresistant, and he's going to sock me!" I shrank inwardly as he stood before me.

Instead of striking me, the stranger extended his hand. He inquired, "Are you a Mennonite, Sir?"

"Yes, I am."

"God bless you, Brother. Let me shake your hand," he cried, pumping my arm enthusiastically. "You're the first one I've ever met."

My eyes must have popped with astonishment. I was at a loss to understand his behavior until he explained, "You see, when we had those terrible storms in Fargo some time back and so many homes were destroyed, the Mennonites came over from Canada and helped the people rebuild. God bless you and your people for what they have done."

"Thank you, Lord, for my Manitoba Russian Mennonite Brethren," I said in my heart.

The stranger led me to his table. "Here, Nels," he introduced, "this gentleman is a Mennonite." He indicated the man addressed as Nels. "This is my cousin, Nelson Wimer. I'm John Diener. We're farmers," he stated, "but we've come into the city to visit our uncle who is a professor at the university. You're coming along with us for dinner." Stunned by this sudden and unexpected turn of events, I paid the bill of the derelict and gladly accompanied my new friends.

Lo and behold, I found myself in the university professor's home and we had food there. I didn't even have to pay for it, and it was much more than a bowl of soup. When train time arrived, the men took me to the station. Oh, it was wonderful!

The wind whistled and howled, and snow whipped about us as I boarded that train for Minnesota. I still lacked sufficient funds for my needs, but Satan's grip had been broken. My God had again demonstrated His faithfulness and His ability to supply my need in the most remarkable and unexpected way. But first He had tried my faith by asking me to share, just as He had with Elijah and the widow of Zarephath. Truly Elijah's God is the same today and answers prayer in the same old way. I believed that then, and I still do.

Money matters slipped from my mind as the train rumbled eastward. Other concerns entered my mind. Would Clayton Drake keep his appointment to meet me at International Falls? Was his desire to find God's will strong enough to cause him to brave the wintry elements of this day: howling blizzards, wind, and snow? Frankly, I would hardly have blamed him if he had given up the whole thing!

However, I had one more layover in western Minnesota before that question would be answered. In spite of my recent experience I was unprepared for the surprises my Lord pressed upon me there.

IV

GOD'S RAVENS

While I praised the Lord for a full stomach, I still did not have grocery money to send Susie. However, it had ceased to worry me. In fact, as I walked out of the depot in western Minnesota in search of a constructive way to occupy my time until the train arrived, I had almost forgotten my lack of funds. My heart continued to overflow with praise for the marvelous way the Lord had moved in meeting my need the previous day.

As I ambled about the village—I don't recall its name—I came across a small building. The construction resembled the hen houses on our Pennsylvania farms, but people with Bibles under their arms were entering it. I decided that it must be a church.

"Saturday night services," I mused. "I've a long wait. I'm going in too."

I stepped into the building. Several men shook hands with me. They inquired my name and where I was from.

"I'm Kenneth Eagle, from near Philadelphia," I informed them. This information alone meant little to them, so I explained, "I'm on my way north to Red Lake, Ontario. Our church is engaged in sharing the Gospel in Red Lake and in the reserves surrounding Red Lake, especially to the north." My companions seemed interested in this information, so I elaborated, "I plan to be flying to several different places, where I will be fellowshiping with recently established congregations. I have to wait several hours for a train and saw your church. I decided to come in and worship with you."

"We're glad you did, Brother," one man responded.

"In what part of Ontario is Red Lake?" an Indian brother asked.

"It's in the northwestern corner," I answered. "It's as far north as you can travel by road, because the road ends at Red Lake."

The eyes of the men reflected surprise. Evidently the idea that a road could end hadn't occurred to them, as it hadn't to me before I had encountered it for myself.

"I know there are Indian reserves up in the provinces," one of the leaders told me. "Are many of them being reached with the Gospel?"

"Our group has outposts at several places," I responded. I went on to explain, "They have the Bible and the knowledge of God, but their faith, in many instances, is just a form of religion and not the faith that results in eternal life."

The taller of my companions noted, "I have heard that witchcraft and devil worship exist among the northern tribes. Is this true, Brother?"

I considered before replying. I did not want to leave a wrong impression. "There has been some of this in the past," I agreed, "and many of the people deplored it. There may still be small 'pockets' where it is practiced, but they are very few."

Another thought struck me. "At the same time," I added, "we also have second generation Christians in some areas—that is, men who know the Lord and have passed this faith on to their children."

"Good, good!" my hosts rejoiced.

"However," I hastened to add, "wherever Christ is not known—right here in your town, or in my home village of Rockydale, or in the North, wherever it happens to be—there is heartache, unhappiness, hopelessness. And in our search for happiness and peace, we turn to all kinds of substitutes."

The faces of my companions sobered. "We see the results of that search in our community, Brother," the taller man remarked. My glance followed his across the street; a man reeled from the door of a tavern and stumbled away. I felt sick to my stomach.

As I stood speaking with the local leader of the congregation, my eyes scanned the gathering flock. It consisted of many Indian people, along with metis and white people. I noticed especially an elderly lady seated near the aisle where we stood talking. I don't know why this particular person stood out in my mind. Perhaps her interest in our conversation caught my attention. Whatever it was, something about her caused me to immediately categorize her as a candidate for salvation. Little did I realize the lesson she would teach me.

The shorter of my companions brought me back to reality by stating positively, "You're preaching for us this evening, aren't you, Brother?"

Appalled at the idea of speaking to this group, although I couldn't quite explain why, I replied, "Oh, no! I really am not. I can't."

"Oh, yes you are," the first man declared. "The Spirit said you should. He told me to invite you to speak to us."

Silently I wondered why the Spirit hadn't told me the same thing! "Really, I don't want to," I insisted. "I just finished a series of meetings in Montana. I'm tired. I'd much rather listen to one of you speak."

"But we aren't ministers," the older man rebutted. "Come, Brother. Why do you think the Lord brought you to us tonight?"

"Am I just being stubborn, Lord?" I questioned. "What would my aged bishop say if he knew I had refused to preach merely because I didn't want to?" Yet I felt strongly that I could not preach and that the Lord did not expect me to.

On the other hand, my presence there in the absence of another ordained man did seem providential, as my hosts insisted. I prayed to the Lord in my distress. "What shall I do, Lord?" I added the urgent request, "If it is Your will, deliver me from this situation."

My "tormentors" relaxed, evidently assured that their case had been won. We all took seats. Mentally I ran through my sermon subjects and outlines; I resigned myself to speaking if no way out appeared. I still firmly believed that the Lord did not plan for me to preach on this particular night.

At 7:25 p.m. two men strode down the aisle. They introduced themselves as ministers from North Dakota. "We are your speakers for the evening," they stated matter-of-factly.

I couldn't resist a mental, "Praise the Lord!"

The men spoke amid frequent echoes of "Amen" and "Praise the Lord" from the assembly. I had never worshiped in a group quite like it, but the Lord, aware of my need at the moment, had chosen this way of supplying it.

The service moved forward. The congregation knelt in prayer. Somewhat to my surprise, different members of the group prayed for "our brother who has speaking engagements in northern Ontario." Across the room to my left, the elderly lady uttered a low-voiced plea which I failed to catch. In my heart I reproached her. "The Lord didn't hear you, you foolish woman," I muttered. Although she did not hear me, the Lord did, and He later set me straight on that subject!

Following the prayer period two men passed the collection plates. After the offering had been blessed, a brother stood to say, "The Holy Spirit told me that we should give this offering to the brother who is going north to fellowship with the believers there."

I could hardly believe my ears.

But that wasn't the end. A sister stood and added, "The Spirit witnessed to my heart, too, that we should do this."

Another brother spoke. "The Spirit also spoke to me. I agree that we should give Brother Eagle this offering."

I sat among that group—complete strangers to me except for our brotherhood in Christ—marveling at the unsearchable riches of our Lord and at His ways which truly are "past finding out."

Well, that love gift from this tiny congregation amounted to $40. How my heart praised the Lord for His faithfulness.

But more followed.

The elderly lady approached me as the meeting closed. "Come, Brother," she invited, and motioned toward a cluttered cabin next door to the church. Wonderingly, I followed her.

She paused with her hand on the latch. "The Lord told me to give you something," she explained, and vanished inside the dwelling.

"You know I have a weight problem, Lord," I sighed

as moments passed. "If it's chocolate cake, I don't want it. I don't need it."

Minutes crept by. I glanced at my watch. I still had time to catch my train. At last my benefactress reappeared bearing a white envelope. She handed it to me. "I have a burden for those people that don't know the Lord," she said feelingly. "God told me to give you this."

That envelope contained a $20 bill.

Stunned, I considered the matter. I had judged my sister, I now realized. I had looked on the outward appearance and had failed to see the heart. I immediately repented and asked forgiveness of my Lord and determined to learn from this experience!

Thoroughly humbled, I reverently placed the money in my pocket. That financially poor woman had recognized that there were others not blessed with a saving knowledge of Jesus. She didn't know who they were or exactly where they were, but God had spoken and she had responded. I thought of the widow and her two mites. Probably my benefactress also had given "all her living."

Glorying in the fact that God's ravens are still in business in supplying the needs of modern day Elijahs, I mailed Susie grocery money and went on my way rejoicing, but with the determination to be more careful in my attitude toward others.

My mind reverted to Clayton Drake as the train rattled eastward toward International Falls. Outside the coach windows the wind whistled, picking up the light, loose snow and driving it to the far corners of the earth, or so it seemed. Had Clayton left the pleasant comfort of home during this holiday season to seek the Lord's will? Was finding God's will that important to him? I wondered.

Thinking of Christmas, just past, reminded me of my own precious family. Tears slipped from my eyes as I thought of that dear group, gathered around the family hearth, sharing the joys of the season. Self-pity threatened as I pondered the sacrifice placed upon me.

Then I recalled the $20 in my pocket. Surely this must have been a tremendous sacrifice to my Indian sister. And sacrifice is, or should be, a normal part of the life of a child of God. And, while some may be called upon to part with money, my area of deprivation seemed to be the lack of a "normal" family life.

A thoroughly chilled figure advanced to greet me as I stepped from the train at International Falls. My joy knew no bounds. In my heart I sensed that the Lord had a special place and work for Clayton Drake, and I was just as eager as he to find it.

Did the people of the Northland offer the key to that question? How should we know? And how would we be sure of the answer when it came?

V

NORTHWARD TO LYNX LAKE

Allen Martz met Clayton and me in the mission plane at International Falls.

With some trepidation I watched as Allen carefully pulled the door shut from the inside after seating himself in the pilot's position. He tied the door with what appeared to me to be binder twine. As the plane lifted aloft, cold air whistled in around that door and also from nicks and cracks in the rattling door on the passenger side. A noisy window caught my attention. A strip of adhesive tape sealed its cracked plastic pane.

Above the roar of the engine Allen asked solicitously, "Are you warm enough?"

"Yes," I replied.

"Are you, Clayton?"

"Oh, yes," our visitor returned, loosening his parka as evidence.

"You see," Allen explained loudly, "we've had to haul some heavy cast iron stoves in this plane, and we've messed up the door seals in getting them in and out. This is why the doors rattle so, and why this latch doesn't work."

I eyed that squeaky door apprehensively. Allen noticed it and grinned.

"Don't worry, Kenneth," he consoled me. "It isn't going to come open. It is almost impossible to open the door of a plane during flight."

I looked doubtfully at the door on my side. I confess that I wondered if Allen knew whereof he spoke!

"Have you ever seen a parachutist jump?" Allen asked over the roar of the engine.

Wondering what connection this could have with our plane, I nodded that I had.

"Hasn't the door on the passenger side always been removed before the plane left the ground?" Allen asked, eyes twinkling.

I remembered a picture I had seen just a few days

before of a fire fighter poised in the gaping door of a plane, prepared to jump. As my mind sorted through what I knew of parachuting, it always came up with that empty space where a door should have been! Allen must be right.

I tried to relax, but my natural curiosity surfaced. I studied the various dials on the instrument panel and wondered what they were. Although the throb of the motor made conversation difficult, I asked anyway.

"Allen, what is this gadget?"

"Oh, that's the gyro horizon indicator, but it doesn't work," Allen replied casually.

"It doesn't!" I cried in consternation, gripping the edge of my seat.

Allen smiled sheepishly. "Don't worry, Kenneth," he comforted. "That instrument is used in blind flying, and we do only visual flying up here."

I breathed a sigh of relief.

"What is that one, Allen?" I inquired, pointing to another dial.

"That is the directional gyro compass. It doesn't work either," Allen answered.

My mind raced. The compass? And it didn't work? How in the world could the pilot get where he wanted to go? What kept him from getting lost? I had to know.

"How can you tell where you're going if the compass doesn't work, Brother Martz?" Clayton leaned forward to ask before I could frame my query.

"This particular compass isn't accurate, Clayton," Allen explained. "Fortunately, we're not that far north. With the aid of a magnetic compass and maps, we get along."

I couldn't rest. I had to know the worst. "Is there anything else on this plane that doesn't work?" I demanded.

A slow grin creased my friend's broad face. "The cylinder head temperature gauge doesn't, and the airspeed indicator isn't accurate," he replied.

I shook my head in disbelief. "Not half of these instruments work," I marveled, "but this plane is flying! Can you tell me how?"

My companion laughed at my discomfort. "Relax,

Kenneth," Allen replied quickly. "You may be flying upon the wings of angels."

I glanced sharply at Allen. Something in his manner assured me he wasn't joking. "What *are* you talking about, Allen? Has anything happened . . .?"

I sensed Clayton Drake, seated behind me, sitting tensely on the edge of his seat. He waited as eagerly as I for an explanation.

"You know, Kenneth," Allen responded, "that we've experienced a tremendous amount of plane trouble due to inadequate repairs." He continued, "I had five forced landings last summer just for that reason. The staff at Headquarters, and Betsy, were very concerned when the plane was out. They usually ran out to watch us land when they heard us coming in, and quite often when we took off too." His voice caught, and he went on. "One time I had an unusually heavy load. I wasn't sure if I could get above the treetops before I got to the end of the lake. Betsy was praying for me as she stood on our dock watching. She saw an angel literally bearing up each wing of the plane until I was safely airborne."

Tears dimmed my eyes. "That is marvelous," Clayton breathed reverently, and I agreed.

"If we could just find a mechanic," Allen sighed. "Bubble gum, adhesive tape, tar, and rags just aren't the best materials to use in repairing planes."

"Bubble gum!" I exploded.

Allen chuckled. "Oh, it's not as foolish as it sounds," he explained. "I punctured a hole in a float out in the bush on one of the docks. The hole wasn't large, but too much water came in for a safe take-off. A little girl volunteered her gum to close the hole. It worked, and we flew it like that for a month or more." I confess that I could hardly believe my ears.

As we winged northward, Allen told us how other makeshift temporary repairs had been made and were allowed to stand entirely too long, simply because the plane couldn't be spared to be flown south to Baudette, Minnesota, for proper repairs.

"We're consulting Curly Mast, a mechanic in Pennsylvania, about helping us find a Cessna 180.

Wiley Martin and I visited him while I was getting my license," Allen went on. "Wiley told Curly that we need a pilot-mechanic badly up here, but Curly didn't respond although he has very willingly repaired several planes for us at various times. I really had hoped that he was the Lord's answer to our need here."

Allen spoke of the time the oil line of his plane sprang a leak while on a flight to Marshy Lake. He had been forced to land on several lakes to replenish the oil before reaching Red Lake.

I had paid little attention to the country beneath us and even less to the time element. Unexpectedly, Allen said, "That is Red Lake below us." He pointed to a village sprawled along the edge of a frozen body of water. The pilot brought the craft down on a cleared area of the frozen lake and taxied up to the wharf.

A new building fronted on the lake. This structure now housed headquarters for Northern Light Gospel Missions, Allen informed us.

"Our living quarters are upstairs," he said. "The office, radio equipment, and supply rooms are on the lower level."

A tall, slender man came out to meet us, wrapped in a snug parka. We clambered out of the plane and walked up onto the wharf. White clouds floated overhead against an intensely blue sky. The air crackled with a vigorous chill. Allen introduced the stranger as Joe Brooks, who lived at Moonsoonie.

We entered Headquarters at dock level. The door opened into a cluttered hall. Various articles, slated for shipment to Moonsoonie, Bear River, and other bush areas, were stacked near the door. Allen led the way through this corridor into a large room to the right which contained several desks and filing cabinets. Windows on two sides fronted on the lake, offering a panoramic view of that expanse of frozen whiteness.

"This is our communications system, Kenneth," Allen announced, showing me an enclosed alcove containing high frequency radio equipment. He smiled, "A brother in Pennsylvania became concerned over the isolation of our bush families, especially during the fall and spring freeze up and thaw, when the planes can't fly. He takes care of the rental on this set."

The radio crackled to life. A voice said, "This is CKQ 153 calling CKQ 457. Come in, CKQ 457."

Allen picked up the speaker and replied, "This is CKQ 457. Come in, CKQ 153. Over."

"Is a plane coming out to Lynx Lake soon? Over."

"Yes," Allen returned. "Someone will bring Kenneth Eagle and a friend out that way as soon as they can leave tomorrow. Over."

"Wonderful!" the voice replied. "Would you send a good supply of first-aid equipment along? We're running short due to a rash of small accidents over the holidays. Over."

"All right," Allen agreed, jotting the items on a note pad in front of him. "Is there anything special that you need? Over."

"No," the nameless voice responded, "just the usual bandages, merthiolate, and adhesive tape. Over."

"Anything else? Over."

"Oh! Yes, you might include a supply of ointment for burns. Over."

"Fine," Allen answered, adding the ointment to the list below the other articles. "Will there be anything else? Over."

"I think that's it," the voice from Lynx Lake replied. "We'll be looking forward to Brother Eagle's visit, and also to meeting his friend. This is CKQ 153; over and out."

This is CKQ 457; over and out," Allen echoed, and replaced the speaker.

"That was Dorothy Lantz from Lynx Lake," he informed us. He grinned quietly, "As you heard, you'll be flying out there tomorrow, Lord willing." A smile crinkled his face. "How do you like this country, Clayton?"

Clayton smiled in return. "I'm not sure yet, Brother Martz."

Before flying us north to Lynx Lake the next day, Allen fitted me with his own parka, an extra one he kept for just such occasions. Fortunately Clayton had come prepared.

We landed on the ice at Lynx Lake after a flight of

ninety minutes. "I'll drop you off at Bear River on the way back," Allen promised me. "You can radio in when you are ready to come out," he instructed Clayton.

Laban and Dorothy Lantz welcomed us at their wharf and invited us into the warmth of their log cabin.

As we stood on the porch of the abode, Laban checked the thermometer. "Whew!" he whistled, surveying the thin red line which already stood low in the tube. "We'll be fortunate if it doesn't drop down to 40 below tonight."

"Forty below zero?" Clayton asked incredulously.

"Right!" Laban returned with a chuckle.

We discovered the next morning just how cold 35 below could be, but I'm ahead of my story.

VI

LEE'S REVELATION

Because the day was still young, Laban loaned us mukluks, a native moosehide footgear, and took us for a walk. We stopped to chat with Lee James and his wife, Elva, in their small cabin. Lee was a tall Indian with a firm jaw and sparkling brown eyes. Following Indian custom, we left our mukluks in the entry and sat cross-legged on the floor, as our host did.

Since Lee understood no English, Laban spoke to him in his native tongue. Clayton and I listened with interest to the unintelligible (to us) conversation.

Laban smiled broadly as Lee uttered a spate of words, chuckled, then ceased talking. We sensed that he waited for Laban to interpret for us so that we also might be included in the conversation. A twinkle gleamed in his eyes as they met ours.

Laban turned to Clayton and me. "Lee has just returned from a preaching trip to the trapping camps," he explained. He smiled at Elva. "Mrs. James was ill when he left. He didn't know if he should go or not, but," Laban gestured, "as you can see, she is well now." Elva smiled in understanding.

"The Lord healed you?" I asked Elva, through Laban. Elva nodded in agreement.

"How long has Lee been a minister?" I asked, my curiosity running high. Our host sat with his back against the log wall of his home, his hands clasped loosely in his lap.

Laban relayed the query to Lee. He replied with a soft flow of words. His expressive eyes communicated with us as Laban translated his part in the conversation.

"He began telling others about Jesus," Laban told us, "as soon as he became a Christian, and began preaching when he came home to Lynx Lake."

"Came home to Lynx Lake?" Clayton asked. I, too, failed to understand.

Laban related our puzzlement to Lee, who considered it, then spoke for several minutes while Laban listened intently. He paused, allowing Laban time to translate for us.

Laban began, "He says he decided to serve Jesus while very ill out in the hospital. He started talking to others in the hospital about Jesus before he came back to Lynx Lake and started to preach."

"Has this been since you arrived here, Laban?" I asked.

"No," Laban replied. "Lee had been preaching for some time when we came in." He turned to Lee, repeating our conversation in Cree. Lee nodded in understanding.

"If you did not lead Lee to the Lord, who did?" I wondered to Laban.

When Laban passed this question on to Lee, a smile crinkled his face. He spoke for several minutes, then paused for Laban to translate.

"He says that his father was a famous medicine man, and deeply involved with witchcraft. Before he died he instructed Lee not to continue in this profession. However, Lee did attend some meetings where these arts were taught but soon realized it wasn't right for him to continue. Finally, it seemed as if someone spoke to him and told him it wasn't right."

As Laban halted, the quiet voice of our host resumed his story. I longed to shift my position on the bare floor, but the moment seemed too sacred for such trivial things, so I sat still. The dignity and character of this man of God impressed us strongly.

"During this time," Laban began after Lee ceased speaking, "Lee was searching but didn't know what for. He attended services at different churches and read the Bible, but it didn't mean much to him. He finally realized that life couldn't be found here."

Lee took up the narrative. At one point he and Elva exchanged gentle smiles of affectionate understanding. He ceased speaking.

"Then he got sick," Laban continued with Lee's account. "Tuberculosis, likely," Laban added, before taking up the translation. "He had to go out to a hospital for over a year. The doctors didn't expect him to live. In fact, Elva received two letters to this effect from the hospital. It was while at the hospital that he decided to follow Jesus. Now the Bible made real sense to him when he read it."

Lee waited patiently while Laban spoke. I thought perhaps his recital had ended. But it hadn't. When he stopped speaking again, Laban continued with the interpretation.

"The Lord showed him clearly," Laban told us, "what was right and what was wrong and how it would be if he refused to follow what was right. Also, one night while Lee was unconscious, he saw Jesus walking ahead of him. His friends and relatives were left behind. This gave him a real burden for them."

Clayton leaned forward with tense concentration. I found myself in the same position. The drama continued. Lee spoke; Laban translated.

"When he returned to Lynx Lake, he talked to the people involved in witchcraft. He told them it wouldn't bring them life, and his testimony halted much of it. However, people began to say he was making up his own religion because he wasn't in an established church." Laban waited. Lee sat thoughtfully.

"How did he handle that?" I asked.

Laban passed my inquiry over to Lee, who smiled in response. He answered, gesturing expressively as he did so. Laban smiled too.

"When the Mennonites came in," Laban explained, "they preached the new birth, so he joined this group."

I thought of Lee's wife Elva, evidently a Christian also. How had it been for her? How had her husband's conversion affected her? I knew that white couples sometimes go through very difficult times before the unsaved partner finds the Lord. Sometimes they never do. How had it been here?

"How was it for Elva?" I probed.

Laban listened closely as Elva responded in a quiet musical voice to his question. He spoke. "Elva says the doctor wrote twice telling her that her husband wouldn't live. It was hard, realizing the children wouldn't see their father again. She thought a lot about death. One night she dreamed that she saw two men come in. One carried a Bible. He asked her what she would do with her life with her husband gone.

"In the days that followed, she thought a lot about changing her way of living and felt for a long time that it would be too hard. Suddenly one day it came to her that it would really be easy."

Elva spoke again briefly while Laban listened with deep concentration.

"Soon Elva also got sick and had to be sent out. It was easier for her, she says," Laban elaborated, "because she had this conviction before Lee came back."

"Have they undergone any persecution?" I asked.

Laban translated the question, and the two flashed me a comradely smile.

"Yes," Laban replied, after listening to Lee's response, "mostly through the children. But when he gets sick, people tell him it is because he has left the old ways. However, the Lord had shown Lee that these things would come; Christ had suffered for Lee, and he in turn would need to suffer for Christ."

We sat in companionable silence for awhile. Presently Lee spoke, spreading his hands wide, and Laban replied.

"He was telling me that the people saw memekweshiwak last night," Laban informed us.

Our blank expressions halted Laban. "Memekweshiwak is a sort of spirit which assumes human form. People who have seen him say he leaves actual footprints," Laban elaborated.

"Did you see him?" I asked Lee through Laban.

Lee shook his head. "No," he returned. "Only unsaved people see him. His appearance brings real fear to the people." He paused thoughtfully, then added, "The people here seem to be searching for a better religion, but they are looking in the wrong direction. Many are very confused."

As I thought of Lee and his conversion—how he came to have the Word—I wondered where it had come from, and how it had ever reached this remote area. As usual, when curiosity gnaws, I asked.

Interest lighted Laban's face as he passed the

question on. "I hadn't thought of that!" he remarked to me, as we awaited our friends' explanation.

Elva and Lee talked between themselves. At last Lee turned to Laban and spoke. Laban translated for Clayton and me.

"Elva tells Lee that her grandmother told her that the Light came in from the coast during the days of her grandmother's youth," Laban stated.

The Light . . . What an interesting way of expressing it, I mused. My mind raced, returning to the latter part of Lee's statement. Her grandmother's grandmother . . . How many years would that be? Clayton interrupted my mental calculations.

"The coast?" he asked wonderingly.

Laban relayed our uncertainties to Lee.

Lee gestured, uttering an explanation which left Laban even more puzzled.

"He says it came in from York Factory—I'm afraid I don't know where *that* is, Brothers—to Big Trout Lake, and spread all over the area from there." Lee's bright eyes watched with friendly interest as we spoke together.

Laban sighed, "I wish I knew my Canadian geography better!"

"Do you have a map of Canada, Laban?" Clayton asked.

"Yes, I do," Laban cried happily. "We'll start back toward the house and see if we can locate some of these places."

Laban rose from his position on the floor. We followed his example. The three of us bade our brother goodbye.

As we stooped to leave the sturdy log dwelling, Laban invited, "Let's head toward home and see if we can find that map, Brothers." We slipped our feet into the borrowed mukluks and trudged through the cold dusk toward the mission house, stopping to chat with people whom we met along the way.

As we tramped along, my mind reverted to Lee and his preaching activity. The realization hit me abruptly: The Lord had raised up a man right here, at Lynx Lake, to share the good news of salvation in Christ. How I praised the Lord! And how I prayed that others would follow.

When we reached the mission house, Laban removed a large map of Canada from a shelf and spread it on the kitchen table. Dorothy joined us in searching for Big Trout Lake and York Factory.

"And the Coast," Clayton added. " 'The Light came in from the coast,' Lee said."

"He motioned toward the east," Laban recalled, moving his attention to that area of the map.

"Here's Big Trout Lake! It's in Ontario," Dorothy cried in delight.

"And way over here on the coast is York Factory!" Laban declared.

"What coast?" Clayton and I demanded in unison.

"The Hudson Bay. See? York Factory is in Manitoba," Laban pointed out, indicating what appeared to be a small town on the map.

"Oh!" I acknowledged. We studied that map. There were no roads and no railroads connecting the areas of York Factory, Big Trout and Lynx Lake. And of a certainty, in the days of Elva's grandmother's grandmother, there would have been no airplanes. How *had* the Light gotten from York Factory to Lynx? And why had the darkness returned?

VII

SLED TRIP

"Say, Brethren," Laban asked that evening as we sat around the heater in the Lantz home, "have either of you ever traveled by dog sled?" Of course neither Clayton nor I had.

"How would you like to try it?" he wondered, glancing from me to Clayton.

Clayton grinned at me and teased, "I'm game, if Brother Eagle is."

Although I had to accept my place as the "old man" in the group, I wasn't about to be outdone. "Surely," I acceded. "I can do anything you young pups can." "Besides," I thought to myself, "what should be so hard about it? The dogs do the work, don't they?"

That night Clayton and I shared a bed. Neither of us slept much. Beyond our sturdy walls echoed the mournful howling of wolves. I had never experienced anything like it. To my ears, they sounded all too near. Mixed with their cries were the excited yelps of the dogs. The discordant symphony of noises hardly served as a sleep-inducing lullaby.

Wonderfully, though, remembering that dark fearful night brings back precious memories. The presence of my Lord was very near during those hours, closer even than the vicious creatures lurking beyond our walls. We sensed His presence right in the room with us. I wouldn't trade that experience for a million dollars.

Laban arose early in preparation for our journey. "We'll be going to the eastern end of Lynx Lake to a trapping camp to conduct services for the people there," he explained. "It is quite a trip," he warned, "but they have no resident minister, and they want to hear the Gospel."

He smiled at his wife. "Dorothy, did you look up our extra sweaters and mittens?"

"Yes," she nodded, indicating a supply of clothing near the stove. "They will be warming up while we eat breakfast. Did you check the thermometer?"

Laban Lantz slipped into a parka, huge fur-lined mittens, and native mukluks. "No," he answered, "not yet." He collected a bucket containing food for the dogs and stepped into the biting cold of a northern dawn.

A short time later Laban returned, and we sat down to a hot breakfast. During the course of the meal, the door opened, admitting two native brethren. Laban introduced them as Andy and Ike Beaver. He and the men conversed briefly. Their somber voices caused us much concern.

After the men departed, Laban turned to Clayton and me, stating, "I'm sorry, Brothers, but we'll have only three dogs for the trip. Brother Andy had promised me the loan of his dog, but he tells me that the wolves got one of his dogs last night, so we'll have only our three dogs, instead of the four I had counted upon."

Clayton and I stared open-mouthed. "You mean . . ." I couldn't bring myself to say the dreadful truth.

"Yes," our host said. "In their hunger the wolves came in and ate one of Andy's dogs. Only his head is left this morning." He paused thoughtfully. "This means," he planned, "that only one person can ride the sled at any time. We'll have to take turns riding and following the sled on foot."

Really, I didn't give too much consideration to his remark. Perhaps, in the novelty of the experience, it didn't occur to me that I would come in for a "turn" following the sled! And the fact that Laban had said that it was "quite a trip" had failed to sink in.

Morning breaks about 8:45 a.m. during the month of December in the Northland. Consequently, our sled trip began around 9:30, just as dawn crept over the bush, bleakly silhouetting the dark, scraggly-topped pines against the pale horizon.

We stepped from the log cabin at Lynx Lake into a scene of postcard beauty. The frost-covered outdoors resembled the inside of a giant refrigerator or freezer. A biting chill hung in the atmosphere of the silent morning. The only sounds were the yapping of the dogs as they awaited departure and the ring of an axe in the distance.

Laban warned, as he led the dogs out to be harnessed, "Here is the sled trail." He pointed to a hard-packed surface vanishing through the bush. "Keep on the trail when you're walking." He grinned wryly. "The snow is almost hip deep off the trail."

"Is that right!" I marveled, studying the countryside. "Constant use must harden the sled runs," I hazarded.

"Yes," Laban agreed. "Walking is fairly easy on the run, but just try getting around out there!" He motioned toward the beautifully landscaped scenery around us.

"No thanks!" Clayton retorted.

The youth and I watched intently as Laban hitched the three dogs to the sled. He deposited our overnight luggage in position, along with our ministerial aids. With the sled packed, Laban glanced at Clayton and me.

"Well, Brethren, are we ready?"

Clayton and I looked at each other. "I guess so." I waited for instructions, expecting Laban to invite our young guest to assume a position on the sled. Instead he gripped the handles of the sled, yelled, "Mush!" and the dogs were off across the snow.

Awkwardly I got my feet in motion to follow the dogs.

I trotted with Clayton and Laban as the dogs raced across the trail. My legs moved automatically, pumping up and down. "This isn't so bad," I decided as the sled slipped through the crisp arctic morning.

The dogs kept to a steady pace, uphill and down, over frozen lakes and muskeg. (Fortunately, the muskeg had frozen before the first snowfall, or we would not have dared to cross it.) We had been traveling for fifteen minutes when the unusual exertion began to tell on me. My heart hammered. Pain flashed through my chest as my heart pounded against my ribs. But the dogs loped steadily forward, unmindful of my aching legs and fluttering pulse.

As my breath came in gasps and my heart throbbed, I suddenly recalled that day years ago when the doctor had examined me for induction into Civilian Public Service during World War II. He had assigned me to

4F classification, due to some abnormality about my heart. Because of my joy at being allowed to remain with my bride, I had scarcely considered the matter. Now, as my heart thumped in my chest, that day returned to haunt me.

"Am I going to have a heart attack?" I shuddered as we dashed past dark spruces and leafless poplars. "Am I going to die in the frozen wilderness?" I had learned through reading that pain in the chest sometimes signals a heart attack.

I thought the situation over as best I could as one foot woodenly moved ahead of the other. "Now don't pity yourself," I scolded, making a conscious effort to trot in an even gait. "Even if you die right now, wouldn't it be better to die here, serving the Lord, than sitting in an overstuffed chair at home?"

After all, I reasoned, I *was* up here in this seemingly lifeless wilderness because my Lord had sent me here. Had I refused to come, I would have disobeyed Him. And He *had* died for me. Was He asking too much in return, should I die for Him?

Graciously my Lord brought Isaiah 40:31 to my mind: "But they that wait upon the Lord shall renew their strength; they shall mount up with wings as eagles; they shall run, and not be weary; and they shall walk, and not faint."

The words of Jimmie Byler, written while on a foot trip with the men on their trap lines, returned to my mind. He had become utterly weary and wondered if he could continue. The Lord seemed to say, "You can still go on, can you not? I have given you all the strength you have. Use every bit of that, then you will receive more as it is needed."

Clinging to my Lord's promise to run and not be weary, I trotted after the sled and, wonderfully, the pain in my chest abated.

Time passed and the miles slipped by beneath us. "Now," Laban said, "you're tired, Brother Eagle. Get on the sled and ride for awhile."

I watched the three dogs struggling up a hill. I thought of the extra effort my 200 pounds would call for if they were to reach the top. "Wait until the terrain changes," I suggested. "Wait until we reach the lake where traveling will be easier for the dogs." That shouldn't be too far, I thought to myself.

Finally we did come to a lake, and with some encouragement from Laban, I flopped exhausted onto the sled. I breathed in great gulps of air.

"No, no!" Laban warned forcefully. "Take short breaths so the air that enters your lungs can warm up. You'll freeze your lungs and get pneumonia by taking all that cold oxygen into your body." He smiled wanly, adding, "The temperature is only 35 below zero this morning." Clayton and I gasped in surprise. It really didn't feel that cold to us.

Laban followed the sled until he too became tired. Clayton and I trotted. Clayton took his turn resting, and I found myself running after the dogs with Laban. As I lifted first one foot and then the other, Laban's statement of the previous evening drifted into my mind, "It's quite a trip," he had said. "That's putting it mildly!" I decided ruefully. When all of us had rested, we gave the dogs a rest also. All of us trotted after the sled.

The journey took three hours. At last we arrived at a moss-chinked cabin on the lake, the site of a trapping camp. People from the surrounding area gathered for fellowship. It thrilled our hearts to hear them sing of their wonderful Saviour. I spoke to the assembly through an interpreter. The congregation gave excellent attention.

Later that day we proceeded to another camp on the edge of the lake. I had never before worshiped under circumstances such as we encountered at this cabin. As we entered the dwelling, we saw a half of the hind quarter of a moose on the floor, with the steak end toward the door. My mouth watered. It lay there throughout the service.

The Christians at this location reminded me strongly of the people Paul met at Berea, in Macedonia. These brethren, without a Scripture in their own tongue, searched the Bible in a related language to see if the things we taught them were true. When references were given, they diligently hunted the verses and checked them. Individuals assured their friends, "Eh heh, that is true. You can believe that."

The reverence of these worshipers impressed me. Just a short time in the past they had been without Christ and without hope. Now they possessed both. Knowledge and freedom from fear through salvation in Christ resulted in a deep reverence for Him. I have seldom seen its equal elsewhere.

I had been too occupied with the physical strain of the journey and my own responsibility to minister the Word to give much attention to Clayton Drake. In fact, I had almost forgotten his purpose in being here. Fortunately, the Lord never wearies and never sleeps, and He had everything arranged and in order.

Just as Laban prepared to dismiss the congregation following the benediction, a mother stepped forward carrying a small baby. She spoke in her native tongue.

Laban faced us as the interpreter translated. Although Laban possessed a fair grip of the language, he had yielded to his Indian brother for these services.

"She says," our brother translated, "that she wants to dedicate the baby to the living God. She says, 'I don't want him to grow up to worship the devil as some of our people still do.' "

Someone behind me broke into heart-wrenching sobs. I turned to find Clayton Drake reaching in his pocket for a handkerchief. As he sought to control his emotion, he said softly, "I feel I ought to remove my shoes. We're on holy ground."

We men placed our hands on that small bundle of possibilities and prayed earnestly that God would bless him and bring him to a saving knowledge of Christ. In our hearts we had the assurance that this prayer would be answered.

"Well, Clayton," I said after most of the group had departed, "has your question been answered? Do you know the Lord's will for you now?"

A radiant smile covered the face of the youth. "Yes, I know." He extended a firm hand. "Thank you for bringing me here, Brother Eagle."

"Thank the Lord, Clayton," I reminded. "He placed the thought in my mind and arranged the circumstances to meet your needs."

"I've had that experience, too," Clayton grinned happily.

I looked at the young man. Intelligent capability seemed to ooze from his manner. My eye took in the homes bordering the lake. I pondered the influence a dedicated Christian teacher could have in this community. Unlimited possibilities flooded my mind.

"The Lord has plans for you, Clayton," I stated, placing an arm over his shoulders. But I had no inkling of how far-reaching those plans would be or of the hurdles to be crossed before they could be brought to fulfillment.

VIII

SURPRISE AT BEAR RIVER

I don't think I've ever been more surprised in my life. But judging from the reaction of others, it must have caught everyone just as unexpectedly as it did me.

Allen Martz flew out to Lynx Lake for us on Monday. He and Clayton discussed the role of education in the Northland as we winged our way into Bear River. Clayton bubbled with enthusiasm and ideas for improving instruction in the local schools. They dropped me off there while Clayton went in to Red Lake to return to school, which had begun without him.

A short, wiry man—Jimmie Byler—met me at the dock and led me up the boardwalk to the house. Upon entering, I found two ladies, one short and stocky, the other quite tall and slender. Both appeared to be in their mid-thirties.

Jimmie introduced the women. Indicating the taller woman, he announced, "Brother Eagle, meet my wife Lydia." Turning to the shorter lady, he explained, "This is our nurse, Mamie Black."

I shook hands with both sisters. Suddenly Jimmie's words registered. "Did I hear you correctly, Jimmie? Did you say . . . your wife?"

Jimmie's black eyes danced with laughter. Lydia's blue ones crinkled with amusement. Mamie chuckled. "Yes, I did, Brother Eagle," Jimmie replied.

I sat down, hard.

"When did this happen?" I inquired, looking at the three of them, "and why didn't anyone tell me?"

"When did what happen?" Jimmie asked innocently.

I couldn't believe my ears. He really acted as if he didn't understand my bewilderment. I decided to be blunt.

"When did you two get married?"

"Oh!" Jimmie exclaimed. He asked, "Don't you read your mail?" His question seemed appropriate. Mamie stood by the post office boxes sorting the mail which

Allen had dropped off when he brought us in.

"Of course I do," I declared, "but no one ever mentioned your marriage, or even that you were going with anyone."

A startled glance shot between husband and wife. Mamie, too, appeared puzzled.

"Well," Jimmie said quietly, "I'm sure I inferred it, Brother Eagle. I signed my last letter 'Jimmie and Lydia Byler,' and I'm sure I mentioned Lydia once or twice."

I couldn't believe it. "Are you sure, Jimmie?" Jimmie nodded. I drew the letter from my pocket and examined it.

Sure enough. There it was in black and white, Jimmie and Lydia Byler. "Well, here it is," I acknowledged, dumbfounded at my oversight.

"Well, how long have you been married?" I asked again.

Lydia smiled gently. "We were married in the fall just before freeze-up, Brother Eagle."

I sensed a spirit of jubilation in the three. "Tell me, Jimmie," I begged. "How did it happen?"

Jimmie smiled broadly at Lydia who returned the smile. "All right, Brother Eagle. We'll tell you about it," he agreed.

"I first met Jimmie in Minnesota," Lydia began, "while I was teaching Bible School at Loman. He came down there to take flying lessons to secure his pilot's license." Her eyes sparkled. "We really gave each other very little attention, due to the obvious differences between us."

"Just how great are those differences?" I asked candidly, tilting my homemade chair back slightly for greater comfort.

"Oh," Jimmie grinned, "a matter of ten years and three inches."

"Is that all?" I quipped.

Mamie smiled. "Brother Allen thought it was enough, Brother Eagle," she stated. "As you know," she continued, "the mission has a policy of carefully screening the young people at the bush stations. We usually have a sizeable age spread between us," she explained. "It helps to minimize problems."

"I understand," I said. "In view of all these blocks and hindrances, how did you manage to get together? You met in Minnesota . . . "

"Yes," Lydia continued. "My brother, Joe Brooks, and his wife were stationed here at Bear River. Our sister Lucy and I came up to visit them. While we were flying out, Brother Martz asked me if I had to go home. Quite frankly, I just didn't want to serve here in the North. I didn't answer him then. But," she smiled at the nurse, "Mamie started on me; when she saw how obstinate I was, she gave up."

"Oh, no, I didn't give up!" Mamie contradicted, as she paused in sorting mail and placing it in the various slots. "I just stopped talking to you and started talking to the Lord instead."

"Did that bring results, Mamie?" I grinned. "Yes," Mamie replied, continuing to tuck letters and other items into pigeonholes.

"The Lord moved by opening my eyes to the need and by showing me how selfish I was in putting my desire to be with my twin sister Lila above Him and His will for me." Lydia smiled contentedly. "It seems silly now, but I cried myself to sleep the night I decided to stay. You see," she added, "my experience as a nurse's aide in the hospital was the one talent I possessed which fitted me in a unique way to serve here. I really was needed."

Mamie stowed the last piece of mail into the proper slot. "I'll get some dinner," she decided, vanishing around the partition separating the two rooms.

"See if you can find something besides yogurt, yeast and molasses, Mamie," Jimmie called jokingly.

Mamie reappeared in the living room. "You see, Brother Eagle," she told me, "our diet up here is extremely limited. If we have the yogurt, brewer's yeast, and blackstrap molasses to supplement our fish and wild meat, we're sure of a balanced diet." She grinned at Jimmie. "The fellows fuss at me but I don't care. Their health happens to be my concern."

"It isn't so bad," the black-haired youth conceded. "At first we hated it, but we've come to rather enjoy it now."

From her position Mamie could see the dock and the path to the house.

"Here comes Sarah James," she remarked, and walked to the door to welcome the elderly Indian mother.

Sarah James sat in the chair Lydia offered her while Mamie checked her mail. Clutching a letter, Sarah continued to sit quietly; local custom forbade disclosing the nature of one's request immediately upon entering the home of a friend.

Jimmie understood this tradition and began speaking to her about things of mutual interest. They conversed in the native dialect. At one point Sarah shook her head negatively. She seemed very despondent.

"She hasn't heard from Tom?" Lydia asked anxiously.

"No," Jimmie answered.

Sarah's soft voice continued.

Jimmie responded.

"She wants us to radio Red Lake and ask if anyone knows anything about Tom," Jimmie told us.

Mamie sighed. "We can try, but the northern lights were playing last night, and that usually messes up the radio," she lamented.

Jimmie went to the radio set and turned a switch. "This is CKQ 345 calling CKQ 457. Come in, CKQ 457."

When he received no answer, Jimmie waited a few minutes and then tried again. Again he received no response to his call. He delayed fifteen minutes before making the third try.

"I'm sorry, but it's no use," he sighed. He repeated this information to Sarah in her language. With sagging shoulders she departed.

"Her oldest son Tom had to go out to Red Lake for minor surgery three weeks ago," Mamie elaborated for me. "He should be home by now, but no one has heard from him since he left the hospital."

I looked perplexed, so Jimmie explained, "You see, Brother Kenneth, once the patient is discharged from the hospital, we have no way of knowing his whereabouts."

I could understand that. We discussed the possibilities of locating Tom James, without reaching any positive conclusions.

Jimmie sat thoughtfully for some time, without speaking. "You know, Brother Eagle," he declared finally, "there was no drinking and little immorality among the Indian people before the arrival of the white man and his firewater."

"Is that right!" I exclaimed.

As Sarah's tired figure plodded dejectedly down the walk, my mind reverted to our previous conversation. I hinted, "You got sidetracked, Lydia. What happened after you decided to stay here at Bear River?"

"Where was I?" Lydia asked, struggling to recall where the interruption had occurred. "Oh, yes, I know. I had just cried myself to sleep after deciding to stay. I asked Lucy to explain to our folks why I was staying, and threw myself into the work here."

I turned to Jimmie. "I was in and out frequently," he added. "Lydia and I got along fine together and we liked each other. It might have ended with that, but . . ."

"But what?" I demanded.

"You see," Lydia backtracked, "I knew that I liked Jimmie a lot. At the same time I was aware of our differences—that I was ten years older and three inches taller than he." She smiled soberly. "I was also old enough not to get a broken heart, so I didn't cherish any dreams or false hopes."

"I can understand that," I agreed. Frustrated, I asked, "What did happen? Evidently something did!"

Lydia chuckled and Jimmie grinned broadly. Lydia resumed her account. "John Ray, a school teacher of another denomination and a real Christian, arrived to teach the day school here on the reserve. He began to show an interest in me. He came over often and helped me do odd jobs or took some of the children and me fishing or took us on nature hikes—things like that." Her eyes sparkled. "Jimmie couldn't stand that. He really got on the ball."

"It certainly opened my eyes," Jimmie declared. "I

didn't lose any time in going after her, once I realized how much she meant to me."

"Mamie was the only person in our entire mission setup who knew what was going on," Lydia informed me, "and she didn't tell."

Lydia paused. In the kitchen Mamie shifted the damper on the wood stove. The fire crackled. A smile of infinite understanding passed between Jimmie and Lydia as she took up the narrative.

"I felt I could not endure a long, drawn-out courtship by correspondence," Lydia stated, "so I told the Lord that if this was His will, to cause Jimmie to come straight out with a proposal." Her face twinkled. "He did."

"We decided to be married very soon because Jimmie was scheduled to go on itinerary for the mission, and we didn't want to be separated," Lydia added. "We've been back only a few weeks."

Mamie came to stand in the doorway. "They've left part of the story out, Brother Eagle," she accused, standing with spoon in hand.

"Oh? What is that, Mamie?"

"Lydia typed an announcement for Brother Martz to post in Headquarters. She gave it to him personally when he came in with supplies. He was speechless; he literally didn't know what to say."

"He just stood there," Lydia put in. "Finally he said, 'That's nice.' "

Jimmie took up the narrative.

"At Red Lake one person would say to another, 'Did you know that Jimmie and Lydia are going to be married?' Inevitably the second person asked, 'Who to?' and the reply would be, 'Why, to each other!' "

"I think," Jimmie spoke reflectively, "that many people had honest doubts about the wisdom of our decision." He smiled happily at Lydia. "I believe they're beginning to think now that perhaps it will turn out all right after all."

IX

JIMMIE'S PROBLEM

"How has the problem of Jay Meekis worked out, Jimmie?" I asked later as the food passed from hand to hand.

"Unfortunately, not too well," Jimmie answered slowly. "I had hoped to mend matters over moving the Sunday school by sawing logs for him to use in repairing his house for the winter. This would serve as rent for using his house for services. I suggested he bring the logs before freeze-up, because the plane would be in then to fly the sawmill back out to Red Lake. It seemed a God-given opportunity to win his friendship."

"What happened?" I asked, settling my bulk more comfortably on the flat-bottomed kitchen chair.

Jimmie thoughtfully cut his meat before replying. "He didn't bring the logs before freeze-up, so I couldn't saw them. Allen came in for the saw, so we dismantled it and flew it out. Almost the very next day Jay appeared to have slats sawed for repairing his cabin." The dark-haired youth grimaced wryly.

"Oh, no!" I cried in dismay.

"He was quite upset," Jimmie said. "I told him I was sorry, but the plane had come for the saw and there was nothing I could do. I couldn't saw slats without a saw. He went away very upset. I didn't know what to expect."

"I wonder why he didn't bring them sooner, Jimmie?" I pondered.

Surprise flashed in Jimmie's eyes. He didn't reply immediately to my question. "You know, Brother Eagle," he said, "I don't believe I even stopped to think about that. I guess I was so ready to condemn him for his behavior that I didn't stop to consider the why's of the way he acted."

"Do you have any idea why he waited so long to come, Jimmie?"

"If I may offer a suggestion, Brother Eagle . . ."

Mamie interrupted.

"Surely," I answered, laying aside my fork and pushing my chair back from the table.

"I think it probably stems from basic cultural differences," she began. "Ours is a time-oriented culture. We live by the calendar and the clock. When six o'clock comes, we get up. We eat breakfast at seven, lunch at twelve, and so it goes, all through the day. We do certain things at certain seasons." We nodded agreement; what Mamie had said was true.

"Jay doesn't operate that way," Mamie explained. "The need of his family regulates his day. The task at hand or the one that needs to be done, is the one he does. If he needs wood, he gets it. If his family needs food, he goes hunting or fishing. During the nice summer weather, Jay's house didn't need fixing because it wasn't cold. However, when fall came . . . "

"I see what you're driving at," Jimmie acknowledged. "I believe you are right, Mamie."

"So the misunderstanding probably grew out of a basic difference in life styles," I conjectured, absently thumping my fingers on the table.

"Yes, I would think so," Jimmie agreed.

"What happened after you couldn't saw the slats, Jimmie?" I probed.

"The next day," Jimmie continued, after refilling my water glass, "I received a letter from Jay. 'You don't wish to help me!' he said, 'so I won't help you.' "

Jimmie paused significantly. I squirmed forward in my chair and searched his face. "What did he mean by that, Jimmie?" I asked.

"You know, Brother Eagle," my friend said thoughtfully, "as I look back upon it, I wonder if I could have helped Jay in some other way. In fact, in view of our recent discussion, I feel I should have offered to help him repair his house by any means of his choice. He may have had some alternative he could have used other than the slats he wanted me to saw." He sighed and added, "It might not have panned out, but at least he couldn't say, as he does now, that I refused to help him."

I nodded my understanding. "What did he mean by

his note, Jimmie?"

"We didn't know at first what he was getting at," Jimmie returned. "Mamie, Lydia, and I discussed it fully but couldn't come up with the answer." Jimmie stopped talking.

"Come on, Jimmie," I pleaded.

Jimmie smiled at my impatience. "When Sunday came, no one came to Sunday school."

"You mean . . ?" I asked hesitantly.

"As chief, he exerts great influence, Brother Eagle," Jimmie responded.

I glanced from Jimmie to Lydia to Mamie. "How do you handle a situation like that, Jimmie?" I challenged.

A sober smile crossed Jimmie's face. "In the only way we know, Brother Eagle," he said crisply. "We prayed. On Monday I visited him. He quite openly acknowledged forbidding the people to come to church. You know," Jimmie stated, turning to face us, "that although many of the people are not born again, they are very religious. They have a smattering of Bible knowledge, take communion when the other missionary comes around, and drink only during the week—never on Sunday, because that is the Lord's day. They feel they are all right and in no need of salvation."

I shook my head in dismay.

The Spirit nudged, "But what of those people at home who go to church on Sunday but do as they please the remainder of the week? Is there really any difference?"

Jimmie interrupted my thoughts. "Jay told me how good he was, and how much he had done for the people since his election, and how carefully he observes all the 'rules.' He felt this entitled him to salvation. I asked him if he had been born again and if Jesus lives in his heart. He wouldn't answer me on that point. He insisted that the Bible teaches we are saved by works, but when I challenged him to show me the passage, he couldn't find it."

"I can see why he couldn't," I responded. "You know, Jimmie, I've been thinking. In our area people tell me of their good moral lives. They think they will be saved because they are honest and don't cheat on their wives or steal from their neighbors." I summarized, "There really isn't much difference in people, is there?"

"Not really," Jimmie answered. "Sin is present in human nature the world over and produces basically the same results."

"Where does the matter stand now?" I inquired.

My host answered cheerfully, "Recently Jay became ill and almost died. Hell opened up before him, and in his words, 'It was hard.' He sent for us. We talked to him, prayed for him, and again pointed him to Christ as his only hope." Jimmie sighed deeply. "Although he has not yet yielded to the Lord, he has reversed his 'no church' stand."

"That's a lot to thank the Lord for," I reasoned, preferring to look on the bright side of the picture.

"Yes," my young friend agreed, "and we're convinced the Lord isn't through with Jay Meekis. I believe he will eventually be won to the Lord."

"That would be wonderful!" I replied, thinking of what the influence of this man could accomplish if used for the Lord.

That evening the four of us sat chatting in the living room. I mentioned Clayton Drake and his call to service. Mamie's face glowed.

"I wonder if he might be the answer," she murmured absently, gazing out across the frozen landscape.

"The answer to what, Mamie?" I prodded.

"Oh, to a dream; no, to a vision I've had," she replied hesitantly.

"Tell us about it," I urged, with a sense of excitement rising in my veins.

"Well, you see," Mamie began, "at present the curriculum is the same in the local schools as it is in Toronto or Winnipeg or Red Lake. The young people here have tremendous ability in using their hands. They ought to have the opportunity to study woodworking, building, carving, or small motor repair—that type of thing—rather than being forced to study algebra, physics, geometry, and ancient history." She felt her way as she spoke. "If we could teach by doing . . . In other words, teach wood crafts by working with wood; motor repair by actually doing this work . . . The academic subjects, such as math, could be coordinated with these projects for the boys . . ."

Mamie's voice trailed off, but we sensed that she had not completed her statement. She resumed, "The girls could be taught skills such as child care, cooking, and sewing. The skills would also be acquired by doing . . . These practical arts would be taught in addition to reading, writing, arithmetic, spelling, etc. Do you see?"

"Yes," I nodded. "That sounds wonderful! But how would it be done? You would need buildings, equipment, teachers . . ."

"Yes," Mamie agreed. "That is the dream I've had." She sat thoughtfully. "If we had the building I visualize, the children could come in from other reserves. While they were here learning these practical skills and crafts, we would also have an opportunity to tell them about Jesus and His love."

"I suggest we pray about it," Jimmie said.

We bowed our heads, and Mamie prayed fervently about this question, this dream she carried in her heart. In my own heart I felt that God would answer.

Her plea turned to another subject. "You know we need a better plane, Lord," she declared. "You know how hard our small planes have been used and how they creak and rattle. I ask that You will send us a better plane, and I thank You for it."

My heart skipped a beat. I sensed that my God would also answer this plea, and I purposed to help Him in any way that I could.

When prayer ceased, I turned to Mamie. "I don't know where it's coming from, Mamie," I said, "but God told me to tell you He's sending you a new plane."

"Good!" Mamie exulted.

"Do you know William Jones, Brother Eagle?" Jimmie inquired.

"I've heard of him. Why?"

"He was up here recently," Jimmie amplified. "Do you know what he called our airplanes?"

"No. What did he?"

"Flying coffins," Jimmie chuckled.

"Flying coffins!" I repeated, aghast. "Are they really that bad, Jimmie?"

Jimmie grinned. "Not really, Brother Eagle. Allen has done a great job in keeping the planes flying. They just sound a lot worse than they really are."

"But William is forming a committee to look into this matter of a plane," Lydia added.

"And we still think we ought to help by reminding the Lord of our need," Mamie concluded.

Mentally, I decided to talk to William Jones.

Today, I thank God for Mamie's vision concerning the school and the plane, and for her prayers which helped to bring about their fulfillment.

However, the black specter of seeming defeat foreshadowed that success. But, I'm ahead of my story. The Lord moved in other areas to answer my pleas for the Northland, and in the most unexpected of ways.

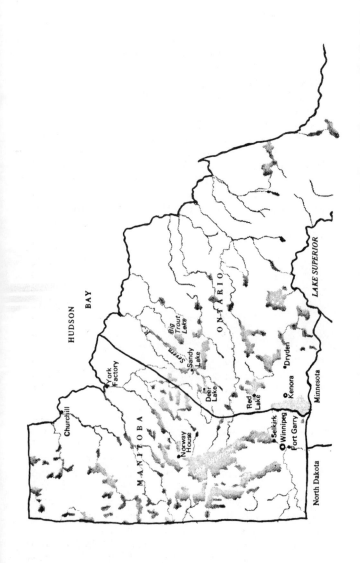

X

"AND, BEHOLDING HIM . . ."

Back at Red Lake as I sat in Allen's lake-front living room, the puzzle of how the Gospel had arrived inland from York Factory returned to haunt me. I pursued the subject with Allen. Happily, he knew the answers.

"This is how it was, Kenneth," Allen stated, leading me to a large wall map of Canada. "White men first came into this area around the Hudson Bay about 300 years ago, but they didn't bring the Gospel. They came for the furs. It was still one hundred years before the Gospel came. The Bay people around York Factory asked for an English chaplain. One was sent over from the old country."

Allen paused reflectively. "I once heard an old Indian, Eli Loon, speak at Christmas on Matt. 4:15, 16." My friend reached for a Bible and read, "The land of Zabulon, and the land of Nephthalim, by the way of the sea, beyond Jordan, Galilee of the Gentiles; The people which sat in darkness saw great light; and to them which sat in the region and shadow of death light is sprung up."

Idly I wondered what connection this Scripture held to the matter at hand. Allen started talking. I wouldn't characterize him as a dramatic speaker, but he certainly caught my attention!

"Old Eli began by describing the Bethlehem hillside. The shepherds were sitting there, watching their sheep. Darkness was all around. Everywhere, darkness." Allen motioned with his hand. I could visualize our Indian brother as he must have gestured in telling this story. "Suddenly," Allen took up the narrative, "a great light was shining. The shepherds were frightened. But an angel spoke, 'Don't be afraid; I'm bringing good news. A Saviour is born.'"

I waited. Allen continued, "Eli went on to say that years ago darkness covered the Northland. There was no hope. The people were without God and without hope. He told how families moved when a child died—as many children did in those times—to escape their grief and sadness; but moving didn't help, so deep was the darkness. Then, suddenly, a great light shone down by the coast . . . "

"That would be the Hudson Bay?" I interrupted to ask eagerly.

"Yes," Allen nodded.

"Go on," I encouraged.

"Down by the coast, beyond the river Severn." Allen smiled. "Eli was still comparing Matthew 4:15, 16 to the North," he explained, and added, " 'by way of the sea, beyond Jordan.' See?"

"I think so," I nodded. I pointed to the map. " 'By way of the sea,' that would be the Hudson Bay, and 'beyond Jordan' would be beyond the Severn River, since Big Trout Lake is southwest of it. Right?"

"Yes."

Allen picked up the story. "From the coast, York Factory, the Gospel spread all over the Northland. It came inland 350 miles to Big Trout Lake, as you are aware, from York Factory." Allen paused tantalizingly. "They didn't have airplanes in those days, Kenneth. How do you think it got to Big Trout? They tell me the missionaries traveled the waterways," and he outlined them on the map as he talked, "cutting across to Norway House by way of this river network." He pinpointed Norway House on the edge of Lake Winnipeg for me. "From here they followed Lake Winnipeg south to Selkirk, and from there went south to Fort Garry, which we now know as Winnipeg. They didn't get into the interior to Big Trout Lake at all."

"Or places like Lynx Lake, I guess," I added.

"Nor Lynx Lake," Allen agreed.

"Well, how did Lee's father get the Bible?" I demanded, scrutinizing the map closely and considering the area separating the two localities.

"Eli went on to tell us that the Christian Indians at York Factory spread the Word all across the North. As persons were converted, they told others. Wherever and whenever contacts were made, the Word spread. People were eager and hungry to hear. It must have been a wonderful time," Allen mused.

"I wonder what happened," I remarked sadly, thinking of the darkness which had returned.

"I'm not sure," Allen answered. The radio crackled to life and our discussion ended.

Several days later I returned to Rockydale to my family. But, although my physical body lived and moved in Pennsylvania, my thoughts and prayers were very much in the Northland.

Susie rejoiced with me over Clayton Drake's discovery. I mused, "I wish we had more men with his talent and ability to serve there."

" 'Pray ye therefore the Lord of the harvest . . . ' " Susie quoted teasingly, but I knew she didn't mean it lightly.

I gathered the breakfast dishes together and carried them to the sink before replying. "I do, Susie, everyday, it seems to me, and I'm still asking Him to send an airplane mechanic up there. It is costing the mission far too much for repairs—money that could be channeled into other areas if we had our own repairman."

Susie paused with a sudsy dishcloth in hand. "It does seem like a legitimate request, Dear. Just wait," she encouraged. "I believe it will be answered."

No premonition of the soul-shattering importance of my trip into eastern Ontario stirred my heart as I left home for a week of meetings in early June, 1959. Perhaps Clayton Drake and his possibilities and plans occupied too much of my mind, leaving small room for speculation into other areas. Whatever the cause, I arrived unprepared.

The beautiful farmland of eastern Ontario reminded me keenly of our own state of Illinois. It contrasted sharply with the Red Lake area, 1200 miles to the northwest. It seemed to be in a different world.

As usual, I received many invitations to eat in homes during the course of the meetings. I enjoyed the fellowship and good food, and the scales showed it. The Lord used my first meal out at Ducksville, Ontario, to begin a strange but thrilling spiritual adventure.

"Brother Eagle," Sister Wagner said as we sat at

dinner that Monday evening, "there is a man in our congregation whom the Lord could use mightily if he would just yield to Him." I didn't pay much attention, I'm sorry to say. I didn't even ask his name.

On Tuesday evening I stood chatting with Brother Zook and Joe Musser, a man crippled by polio, but who nevertheless bore a shining testimony for his Lord. Joe said, "You know, Brother Eagle, there is a man in this congregation whom the Lord could use mightily if he would just yield to Him."

"Have you been talking to Sister Wagner?" I asked casually.

"No, why?" he asked in complete innocence.

"I just wondered," I said, without offering an explanation, and Joe asked for none.

Surprisingly enough, my own experience of "double revelation"* somehow did not enter my mind, devastating as it had been. Had it occurred to me, I might not have needed a third prodding from the Lord to wake me up.

The Lord saw fit to catch my attention by repetition. Wednesday evening I dined with the Zehr family. Brother Zehr knew nothing of the two previous conversations. Following the meal as we sat in the den of their home, he said, "Brother Eagle, there is a man in our congregation whom the Lord could really use if he would just yield to Him."

I thought, "That's the *third* time I've heard that. Lord, are you trying to tell me something?"

"Who is he?" I inquired without much real interest.

"His name is Royal Fretz. He is a young man, and he always sits on the back bench, but he doesn't often attend evening meetings, so he probably won't be at these services. However, he is a church member, but he isn't as consecrated as he should be." He paused briefly, and I waited. He added, "He operates a very successful shoe factory, engaged in the manufacture of baby shoes. Some of our largest mail order houses carry his products."

"Really?" Interest began gnawing in my mind. But, although I sensed the Lord's hand in this matter, the spiritual plight of Royal Fretz left me cold and unstirred. The Lord set about changing this.

That night I stood as usual before the congregation to deliver my message. I had become accustomed to seeing each night many of the one hundred faces before me, and recognized a few of the new ones. None of these made any special impression, but as I spoke, something happened; something that I had never experienced before in my preaching ministry.

Suddenly, from out of that group of people I sensed someone staring at me, watching me intently. I can't explain it, but I knew that somewhere in that audience someone was giving me much more than average scrutiny. My mind told me that this individual sat somewhere to my right near the back of the church. Without seeming to be obvious, I focused my eyes on the area from which I felt that strange intent look originated. It came from a man on the back bench near the door. I recognized him as Royal Fretz. My heart was touched. I thought of Jesus and the rich young ruler. "And he, beholding him, loved him . . . ," and that very night at that very moment was born in my heart a feeling for Royal that I can't describe.

God gave me a burden for Royal Fretz. He said to me, not with the hearing of the ear but through the understanding of the heart, "Speak to him; I have a great work for him to do." I battled the issue in my mind as I gave the invitation and closed the service. "I can't, Lord," I hedged. "He'd never listen to me. I'm Bootlegger Ralph's Brat. Remember?"

No one responded to the invitation that evening, although I waited hopefully, thinking that perhaps Royal would come forward. He didn't. There had been no response on the previous evenings. Somewhat let down, I accompanied Brother Zook to the door to greet the congregation as they departed. I noticed Royal and his wife Margaret in the line back of us as they waited for people to move out.

"The Lord bless you, Sister Wagner," I said as she passed us, assuring us of her prayers.

Joe Musser came next. I greeted him by name and told him what an encouragement his faithful presence was to me.

Teenaged sisters, Lola and Dotty Good, walked through the line and shook hands. They reminded me of my own sisters, Nancy and Ellen, in their younger years. Their names had not been hard to keep.**

More people flowed through the door. Many of them I recognized and greeted by name. At last Royal Fretz and Margaret stood before me. In spite of myself tears stood in my eyes as I said, "It's good to have you here, Royal. I've heard of you and your shoe factory."

"Come around and visit the factory," the young man invited.

"Thank you. I will if I can find the time," I said gripping his hand firmly. Mentally I determined to make the time.

Joe Roach, a friend of Royal's, followed behind him. I recalled what I had learned of his history. Brother Zook declared that Joe and Royal had served the devil together. In recent years Joe had made an all-out commitment to the Lord, but Royal was lagging. "I know that Joe is deeply concerned about Royal," Brother Zook told me. "He was talking to me about it just last evening."

The memory of this dapper, handsome, impeccably dressed, and fine looking young man went with me to the parsonage that night.

I wrestled until one o'clock with my God. "Speak to Royal. I have a great work for him to do," the Lord insisted.

"I can't, Lord," I rebutted. "Can't You see? He comes from a good family. He has all the marks of excellent family background." I strode across the floor to the window. "And he has class, Lord! That bow tie! Did You notice that? And the cut of his suit? And his hair, how it was combed? Not one hair out of place! I couldn't come up to that, Lord, in a hundred years!"

"I'm not asking you to be like him in manner or dress," my Lord persisted. "I just want you to speak to him about his relationship to Me. I have a great work for him to do."

I stood at the window. Sweat poured off my body. I walked frantically back and forth across the floor. "I can't do it, Lord!" I cried. "Our backgrounds are too different. What does he know of bootleggers and outlaws and penny pinching? He wouldn't listen to a country bum like me." I reminded the Lord again, in case He had forgotten (although I knew He hadn't), "I'm Bootlegger Ralph's Brat, don't forget."

"I haven't forgotten," my Lord seemed to reply, "but *you* tend to forget. He was a bootlegger, saved by my grace. Speak to Royal Fretz!"

Satan's hold was too firm. "I can't do it, Lord," I moaned.

At 1 a.m. I dropped into an exhausted sleep. I looked in vain for Royal's presence on Thursday night and Friday. On Saturday morning Brother Zook took me to visit the shoe factory. Royal welcomed us heartily. His extremely tidy appearance, even in work clothes, only strengthened my fear that a wide cultural gap would hinder spiritual communication.

"I've been sick all week," Royal explained as he led the way through the shop. "That's why I haven't been back to the meetings." He grinned ruefully. "I'm head laster, shipper, paymaster, and salesman of this operation, and I've been shot until evening." I could believe it. His face provided ample evidence of his physical illness.

We prepared to leave. My heart ached. I couldn't leave this young man so dear to my heart without one word of encouragement. I tried to speak. Tears choked my voice. In spite of a tremendous effort to control myself, I fell on his shoulder and wept.

Surprisingly, Royal didn't seem to be embarrassed. At last I pulled myself together enough to say, "The Lord needs you, Roy." I noticed his natty bow tie, tweaked it playfully, and added, "He's calling you, in spite of this thing."

Royal grinned at me and gripped my hand with a firm clasp. Somehow, that handshake sealed an unspoken bond between us.

I left the factory heavy-hearted. So much needed to be said, but hadn't been, and I knew I couldn't say it. I just wasn't equipped to, either by background or training. Royal Fretz, I told myself, was a man completely out of my class.

Royal failed to appear at the service on Saturday night, nor had I expected him to. Still, I felt a twinge of disappointment. My gloom deepened when no one came forward during the invitational hymn. But, unknown to me then, that night's battle had just begun.

Royal Fretz descended heavily upon my heart as I returned to my room that Saturday night. "Speak to him!" my Lord commanded again. "Speak to Royal Fretz. I have a great work for him to do in the Northland."

The burden lay heavy on my heart. I thought of this able, talented young man, of his magnetic personality, and of his ability to work with his hands. I considered his usefulness to the mission at Red Lake, and the place he could fill. I knew now why three different persons had spoken to me of his possibilities.

My burden grew as I pondered what the Lord had revealed to me. I felt that I had to seek Royal Fretz out, wherever he lived in that area; I must tell him that God was calling him, asking him to dedicate his life to Him, to give everything to Him on the altar of sacrifice.

But my uncultured, seedy background rose up to haunt me. "I can't do it, Lord," I cried in anguish. "I can't speak to him. Don't You understand? He'd never listen to me. I'm too far below him."

"Let Me be the judge of that," the Lord told me. "I want you to speak to him. I'm calling him to answer the cry for someone to come and teach them about Me. Speak to Royal."

The battle raged until nearly dawn, but I couldn't bring myself to agree to speak to this man. "Lord," I cried, "if You want someone to speak to him, You'll have to tell someone else. I can't."

But that didn't settle the matter! Truly, God is merciful. He gave His rebellious child a second (or was it a third?) opportunity.

*See *Cry of the Northland.*
**Royal later said that Brother Eagle's ability to remember names, here illustrated, is one thing that impressed him. "It was the man, more than his preaching," is Royal's testimony.

XI

THIRD OPPORTUNITY

"God moves in a mysterious way, His wonders to perform." How true that song is! I never cease to marvel at the way He works. And the operation of His hand where Royal Fretz was concerned . . . Well, let me tell you about it.

The telephone rang in the Zook home about 8 a.m. on Sunday. "Long distance calling person to person for Kenneth Eagle," Brother Zook announced as he handed me the instrument.

"Oh, I do hope nothing is wrong," I fretted, accepting the call.

"Kenneth," Susie's voice came to me clearly over the miles separating us, "Luke is very ill. Please hurry home." My heart almost stopped beating.

"Immediately?"

"No," she replied. "Finish out your meetings tonight, but don't linger to visit with friends or spend any extra time. Just start home as soon as the service is over."

"All right, Dear. What is wrong with Luke?"

"He has a severe chest cold, bordering on pneumonia. Please pray for us, Kenneth," my wife admonished.

"Of course, and I'll come as soon as I can get there," I promised, replacing the telephone.

I relayed this information to Pastor Zook. His eyes mirrored sympathy as he scanned the breakfast table, surrounded by his own healthy brood.

"I understand how you feel, Brother Eagle," he said, passing me the cream for my coffee. He pondered a moment, excused himself from the table, and returned to the telephone where he made several calls.

"It's all arranged, Brother," he informed me happily. "You're not taking a poky old train home tonight. I've arranged for Joe Roach to drive you to London to the airport. I've also made reservations on a flight into Philadelphia for you."

Relief and gratitude brought tears to my eyes.

That evening before the service began, Brother Zook stated, "I'll close the meeting for you and have the benediction. Joe will be waiting for you in the anteroom to take you to the airport, and may the Lord bless you."

I preached the closing sermon of those meetings and gave the invitation. Everyone remained glued to his seat. Tired, depressed, discouraged, and with tears streaming down my cheeks, I walked down the aisle toward the rear of the building.

Joe stepped forward as I approached the anteroom.

"You're taking me to the airport, Joe?"

"Yes."

I reached for my hat and we started toward the outer door of the church. A young man almost collided with us. It was Royal Fretz!

"Where are you going, Joe?" he demanded.

"I'm taking this minister to the London airport. Come on; you're going along with us," Joe invited.

Royal rubbed his stomach tenderly. "Oh, no. Not me; I'm sick. I only came tonight because Margaret insisted."

Joe cast a steady glance on Royal. "Now look, Roy," he reasoned soberly, "you promised me this morning when I called you that you would go along." He added forcefully, "It's going to put a strain on our friendship if you back out now."

"Oh, all right," Royal conceded. "I'll go, even if it kills me. Let me tell Margaret first."

We climbed into Joe's car, he and Royal in the front and I in the back. Joe paused a moment before starting the car. Something prompted me to place a hand on Royal's shoulder and ask, "Are you really ill, Brother?"

"I have a bad case of stomach cramps, Brother Eagle," he explained.

I considered how such an illness could complicate our trip. "Do you mind if I lay hands on you in the name of Jesus and ask Him to heal you, as Mark 16 directs?"

If my request startled Royal, he surely didn't show it. "Not at all. Please do."

As I had prayed for Joyce, my baby daughter, some years before, I now placed my hand upon the shoulder of my dear brother and asked for his healing in the name of Jesus. And, as the Lord had touched the body of our daughter and healed her, so He also touched the body of Royal Fretz.

Holy silence reigned for some time as Joe drove toward London, Ontario. At last Royal remarked in awe, "I didn't know the name of Jesus had such power, Brother Eagle."

His words reminded me of something and someone, an experience in the early days of my ministry. "I've heard someone else say that very thing, Royal. He was a young minister in Kentucky. We were dealing with a witch who . . . "

"A witch, did you say?" Royal interrupted.

"Yes," I replied, and beginning with the sticks poked through the weather boarding cracks, I related the entire episode: the rain which came in response to a brother's prayer, forcing the trouble makers inside, and continuing the narrative right down to Ginger and her enchantments. My audience listened spellbound.

When I paused, mentally comparing the fruitfulness of those services to the apparent lack of it in this series, Royal asked, "How do you feel about these meetings, Brother Eagle?"

"Oh, Brother," I answered with tears in my voice, "not one person responded. I might just as well have stayed home. In fact," I added, "if I could find a cave, I'd crawl into it, like Elijah did."

Royal's next words took me by surprise. "I've been helped," he declared, "even if no one else was. The Lord has been speaking to me."

I placed a trembling hand on his shoulder. Oblivious to the street lights flashing by as we passed through the outskirts of the city, I said, "The Lord has been speaking to me about you, too, Royal."

The young man turned to face me. "He has! What did He say to you?"

Seriously, but with deep earnestness and love, I answered, "He says He has a great work for you to do if you'll only yield to Him."

Great sobs shook the body of the young man before me. Joe drove silently. I waited.

At last he began talking. "The Lord spoke to Margaret and me years ago about going into the ministry, but we put Him off. We had a huge debt, $40,000, to be exact. We promised the Lord when we got that paid, we would get some training for His service, but we didn't do it. We tried to still our restlessness in all kinds of ways. That's why I'm in the shoe business. We thought a steady job with a more normal life might help."

Joe maneuvered the car into the airport parking lot and cut the switch.

"It hasn't worked, has it, Brother?" I probed gently.

"No," Royal replied fervently. He faced me. "Brother Eagle," he declared, "I'm ready to yield tonight. If the Lord wants me to give up the shoe factory and preach, I'm ready to do it. If He wants me to serve Him here, or somewhere across the province, I'm ready to do that, too."

Royal paused. Joe and I waited. "You know, Brother Eagle, all week it has seemed as if an unnatural force has been oppressing me, trying to hinder me. I decided this evening to defy it and come to this meeting even if it killed me. Now, since I have reached this decision, that oppressive force is gone."

"Praise the Lord!" I cried.

Oh, how my heart rejoiced as my brother made an altar there in the car, rededicating and reconsecrating himself fully to the Lord, with no strings attached.

As we trod joyfully toward the ticket office, Royal spoke, "Brother Kenneth"—we were on a first name basis now—"do you have a suggestion for a useful vacation this summer? I know that I won't be satisfied now just to go somewhere and fritter away my time and money. I want this vacation to glorify my Lord."

I can't tell you how my heart sang praises to my wonderful Lord. "Why don't you write to Allen Martz at Red Lake, Roy? They can always use Bible school teachers up there. I can't think of a better way to have a useful vacation."

"I'll do that," Royal declared. "I'll do it yet tonight."

"Better check with Margaret first," I cautioned, placing a hand on his arm. "She should have a say, too."

Royal's face clouded; in a moment it cleared into a smile. "I believe she'll agree," he said. "She's been after me for a long time to do things differently."

Joe picked up my suitcase, and we found our way to the plane. I boarded it, never expecting to see Royal Fretz again.

That experience has taught me a valuable lesson. Although those meetings appeared fruitless, humanly speaking, yet they were extremely productive from a long-range view. My job, I realized now, is to sow the seed. The results are up to Him.

Well, I received a letter from Royal about two weeks after my return home. I quote in part: "You know, my dear Brother, I must tell you that God has been especially sweet to me the last week or so. I suppose it is because I have again received a proper perspective on life. I must not leave the impression that God has not meant much to me before, but rather since the meetings and especially, since our fellowship last Sunday night." My, how I rejoiced.

Roy went on. "My beloved wife and I have cast our lives at the Lord's disposal, and I must confess that since we have told the Lord that we are willing to go anywhere He leads, life has new meaning."

A few items followed, including the fact that he had indeed written to Allen Martz. He wrote further, "I must tell you that we have established a time of special prayer and meditation, from six to seven in the morning. God has richly blessed us in this experience and we thank Him for it. But this is the message I wish to convey to you, that even if we are separated by international boundaries and miles of country, we are praying for you every morning between six and seven, and God willing, will continue to lift you before the mercy seat of God."

Tears blurred my eyes. I shook my head in exasperation. More followed. " . . . I feel this is my duty because Jesus blessed me so much through your testimony, and we experienced so much of the love of God through your ministry . . . "

Humbled beyond words, I bowed my head in praise to God. This, from a brother whom I had told the Lord repeatedly that I couldn't talk to because he wouldn't listen to me! And even then, my Lord had been forced to circumvent my stubbornness and place me in a situation where I had little choice before I followed His direction.

Fortunately for me, my Lord's longsuffering and kindness are great. I shudder to think what the consequences to the mission, and to Royal, would have been had not the Lord overruled my "I can't."

But, I'm sorry to say, I didn't fully learn my lesson. All too soon I found myself again saying, "I can't," and the Lord had to use a hard lesson to teach me. But I'm ahead of my story. I must revert to Clayton Drake and some other items before telling you of that experience.

XII

ANSWERING THE CRY

I rejoiced when news came to me from Clayton Drake. Following his graduation from college, he moved to Red Lake to start his teaching career. He also married Zola Mast, a fine Christian lady whom he had met the previous year.

I also received a letter from Royal Fretz, postmarked from Red Lake. I opened it eagerly. He wrote, "I have often been reminded of what you told us about Red Lake. You know, Brother, we have had some rich experiences of the grace of God. How wonderful a miracle the Lord of hosts has wrought in the lives of men! My heart is thrilled that we who are born again, and know what it means to be a disciple of Christ, can bow our heads and worship Jesus together—they in their native tongue, and I in mine. Kenneth, the Lord has led me to see that this is where He wants us. How can we neglect to do His will?"

Both Royal and Margaret were teaching; he, young people twelve to sixteen years of age, and she, the smaller children. Their own small sons also attended the schools.

The closing words of Royal's letter expressed my own feelings neatly. "I shudder to think what I would have missed out on had you not encouraged us to go to Red Lake. You know, Brother, I left my heart there." I trembled more with the thought of what the results would have been had the Lord not overruled my stubbornness. Would Royal be a spiritually alive person as he is now, I wondered? No one can say positively, I'm sure. My only concern, as I considered the matter, was to be certain that I am open to hear, and ready to obey, when my Lord gives my next set of directions!

Time passed. One Saturday in January I placed Luke on a kitchen stool and started to cut his hair. The mail man deposited our mail in the box and Michael brought it in. It hardly seemed possible that our oldest son had graduated from high school. He had found full time employment in hopes of entering Bible school. Susie and I had agreed to furnish his clothing and other incidentals if he took care of tuition charges. Michael watched the mails regularly for a reply from his application form sent to an eastern Bible school.

"Did it come, Son?" I asked over the top of Luke's blonde head.

"No, but a letter from Jimmie Byler did," Michael answered.

"Read it for me, Michael," I requested, running the clippers up the back of Luke's neck.

Michael glanced at the clock. "Sorry, Dad, but I don't have time. I have to be at work in fifteen minutes."

Susie took the letter. "I'll read it, Dear. I have time, and I enjoy Jimmie's letters as much as you do."

"Dear Kenneth," Susie began. "The presence of Clayton and Zola Drake here at Bear River has been a real blessing to all of us. Clayton is a master teacher; he really puts his heart into his work. We see his light until 1 a.m. many times as he works to prepare his lessons for the next day, if for some reason we need to be up at that hour. The parents tell us the children are learning well."

Susie smiled happily at me. "The Lord has plans for Clayton, Susie," I declared. "This is just the beginning."

Susie grinned impulsively at me. "Doesn't He have plans for *all* of us, Kenneth?"

"Of course, Susie, but . . . " I gave up. "You know what I mean. What else does Jimmie write?"

Susie resumed the letter. "Lydia reports real spiritual growth in Beulah, the mother who was healed because of the faith of her son Joel. She has experienced some real struggles (who of us does not?) but is gaining spiritual strength through them. Beulah is so happy to be free of the fear and superstition which have bound her for so long."

"What is superstition, Dad?" Luke asked.

"Did you ever hear anyone say that you will have bad

luck when Friday comes on the thirteenth day of the month?" I asked.

"Yes, I believe I have," my son answered.

"Well, that is a superstition."

"Some people say that if you break a mirror, you'll have seven years of bad luck," Susie added.

"Or if you trim your fingernails on Sunday, the devil will be after you all week," I enlarged, remembering one of Dad's favorites during his unsaved days. "After I was converted, I saw how foolish that was," I told my son. "Satan was after me all week, no matter when I trimmed my nails."

"Does that give you some idea of what superstition is, Luke?" Susie asked.

"Yes," he concluded, "it's something people are afraid of that you don't need to be afraid of."

"That's a pretty good definition, Son," I decided. "Let's proceed with the letter, Susie."

"I must tell you of Peter," Jimmie continued. "You recall that I told you of joining Peter and his brother Sam on their trap line, don't you? Recently Peter accepted Christ as his Saviour. We had spoken to him a number of times over the last several years about God's love for him, but he always rejected it. One Sunday recently he became quite angry at me during the preaching service. He thought I was preaching about him. The Holy Spirit had taken what I said and applied it to his heart."

My thoughts wandered from the letter as I recalled my own experience. I had been positive that someone had "tipped off" the preacher the night I was converted. What he said during that service fit my situation so exactly!

" . . . go anywhere now, he says," my wife read. I realized with a jolt that Susie had continued reading while I had been "wool gathering."

"I'm sorry, Dear," I interrupted her. "Backtrack a little. I missed something; my mind wandered."

"Where was I before you left me?" Susie asked with a twinkle.

"Peter had left the service angry."

"Oh, all right. I'll start there, then," Susie decided.

" . . . He thought I was preaching about him," she read. "The Holy Spirit had taken what I said and applied it to his heart. When he finally yielded to the Lord, he was so happy he didn't sleep for two days. He told anyone who would listen what the Lord had done for him. He can go anywhere now, he says. Before, he was afraid something might happen to him. He says he can sleep now. In his sinful condition he was fearful of dying while unconscious. We believe this man is being groomed for a place of responsibility in the emerging church here at Bear River."

"That's interesting, Susie," I remarked as my wife paused. "I recall how I, too, dreaded the unconsciousness of sleep. What if an earthquake should strike, and we should all be killed? Or what if the house should burn down, and none of us get out? Anything could happen during those hours of darkness . . . "

Susie nodded in understanding. "Praise the Lord, it's different now, though," she reminded.

"Yes," I agreed, "it certainly is." Susie's attention returned to Jimmy's letter.

"Last week," she read, "I was called upon to speak at the funeral of Lolly White, an 82-year-old neighbor. She and six others had wandered out in sub-zero weather. They were lost two days and two nights before their bodies were found. Lolly had heard the message often. As I stood beside that lifeless body, I asked myself, "Am I looking at a body whose soul may be in hell? Do I really believe this? Do I realize as I speak of the love of Jesus that some listening soul may be at the brink of hell? Could this be their last warning? Kenneth, it really shook me!"

Susie stopped thoughtfully. "That would be terrible," she breathed, "freezing to death!"

"But it happens occasionally," I said sadly. "Sometimes someone starts from one place to another, not realizing how cold it is, or someone may lose his way and freeze before getting to shelter."

"In our area," Susie mused, "people start out in their cars and have automobile accidents and get killed."

"Yes," I agreed, "but we are so accustomed to it that it doesn't strike us as anything so terrible. Really, I expect a lot more people lose their lives through alcohol on our highways than freeze to death in the Northland . . . "

"But because it is an everyday occurrence, we shrug it off," my wife interrupted.

"Right!"

"Well, there is more," Susie replied.

Picking up the letter, Susie read on, "Sunday night the trader's wife arrived without a coat and with just one shoe. The thermometer stood at 52 degrees below zero. She carried their little girl, who had convulsions and a bad cold."

"Fifty-two below zero and no coat!" Susie cried. "How did she ever make it? What kept her from freezing, with only one shoe?"

"Evidently it wasn't far," I replied. My clippers had again ceased work. "Let's just listen to Mother read, Luke," I suggested, "then I'll finish your hair."

My mind reverted to the subject of temperatures. "Laban Lantz says your ears will freeze in less than five minutes at 40 below if they are unprotected," I informed Susie.

Susie returned to reading. "I stopped to chat with Johnny Keene today, Kenneth. Did you ever meet him? Johnny has been paralyzed in his back for years, but this does not handicap him, if you understand what I mean. Do you know what I found Johnny doing today? He sat on the floor, teaching his ten-year-old son Abel to make rabbit snares. After Abel mastered the art of making the tool, Johnny meticulously instructed him in the art of setting the snare.

"Several weeks ago I stopped in to visit Johnny, and he was showing Abel how to handle a gun and teaching him the secrets of stalking game. He is such a cheerful person it is a joy to visit him."

The letter ran on. "I had to think, Brother Eagle, of the many things Abel is learning from his father that Johnny is probably unaware of—patience in the face of adversity, perseverance, and discipline. What an example for good his life will be! And what an example that lad has to live up to! I praise God for Johnny Keene."

"Is Johnny a Christian, Dear?" I queried.

"Jimmie doesn't say," Susie replied.

"But what he says is true, Susie, even if Johnny isn't a Christian. It reminds me of a poem I saw once. It said something about seeing a sermon rather than hearing one—how much more valuable a person's life is in showing us how to live than his words alone are. Too often our deeds speak so loudly that others can't hear our words. They have no difficulty understanding what we do and are."

"That is true," Susie agreed thoughtfully.

"Well, let's get on with the remainder of this missive," my wife suggested. "Recently Sam Loon came over and asked us to pray for his daughter who was very ill. Of course, here at Bear River we are ninety miles from a doctor, and the child was too far away to bring in, or for us to go to it. Together we prayed that the Lord would heal her, and He did. Samuel returned later to tell us what the Lord had done, and we praised Him together.

"Lydia's brother Joe at Moonsoonie reports real enthusiasm there. Lately a ten-hour period of Bible study for new Christians was interrupted only long enough to eat. This glorious event took place after five days of unscheduled visitation by two brethren—Jim Cook, from Stormy Lake, and Moses Loon, from Snowshoe Falls."

Jimmie added, "I must tell you about Moses Loon, Brother Kenneth. I met him on a trip into Snowshoe Falls last summer. We talked about the Lord, and he told me of his conversion.

"Moses grew up at Stormy Lake. His parents both died when he was small so an uncle, who was a minister, raised him. This uncle taught him to trap animals, set snares, and many other skills. At that time, about 1919, the family lived in a tent.

"I asked," Jimmie elaborated, "if they lived in the tent year round. Moses replied that they did. I wondered how they kept warm during the winter. Moses replied that they packed moss against the outside of the tent. This served as insulation. In addition, the family slept on rabbit-fur blankets, and used moose-hide covers, topped with canvas. Also, there were ten children in the family, and they helped to keep each other warm.

"Moses tells me," Jimmie added, "that the people began to build houses with moss on top about fifty years ago. Now other types of roofing are used."

Jimmie returned to Moses' spiritual pilgrimage. "Moses' uncle taught him the Ten Commandments and not to work on Sunday, but Moses didn't keep those commandments. He heard the Bible read, but he didn't understand it; it didn't make sense to him. He took part in communion services, but no one explained the meaning of the emblems to him. A birthday dance followed this ceremony, and Moses joined this activity.

"Moses told me they heard that missionaries had come in to Snowshoe Falls with the Gospel, but no one ever came down to Stormy to tell them the Good News. Finally, a brother came to them from Snowshoe Falls. He started talking. He talked for a week, but no one listened."

Susie and I looked at each other. I was thinking that I probably would have given up and gone home. Evidently our Indian brother had not.

"He talked for a second week," Jimmie continued, "and Moses began to listen and to understand. He accepted Jesus as his Saviour. He says now that his head must have been about s-o-o-o thick, and he spreads his hands wide, while a happy smile covers his face. I hope you will meet Moses sometime, Kenneth."

"Just one more page," Susie reported, flipping through the sheets in her hand.

"As usual," Jimmie went on to say, "when things begin to move for God, Satan also gets busy. Joe tells us that Satan has made himself manifest, to use his terminology, in person on several occasions to believers at Moonsoonie. He naturally chose the appearance to be in the form of a white man carrying a sword, since the Canadian Indians refer to Americans as Big-Knife-Men. Satan is a cunning adversary."

Susie gasped. I remembered Lee James and his story of how the people at Lynx Lake had seen a spirit, but there only unbelievers had seen it. I told Susie about this.

"There is a little more," Susie said in a small voice, as though she dreaded what the remainder of the letter might hold.

"I should say yet," Jimmie concluded, "that those who witnessed these appearances tell us Satan can make himself disappear at will and that he can also walk without leaving or making tracks. You will probably find these things hard to believe, Brother Kenneth, but they do happen here.

"Our only strength in the face of such evidence is the knowledge that Satan was defeated by the empty tomb! 'Greater is He that is in you than He that is in the world.' Thank God, and pray for us. Jimmie and Lydia Byler."

Slowly Susie returned the letter to its envelope. "I wonder why we don't experience such occurrences," she mused.

"I don't know," I answered thoughtfully. "I hadn't really considered it."

"What's this letter, Dad?" Luke asked, picking up an unopened envelope which had been neglectd.

My heart skipped a beat when I saw the Ontario postmark, but it proved to be a strange one. The letter invited me to conduct a series of meetings at Pickway, Ontario. Filled with excitement at the prospect of perhaps getting close enough to the Fretzes for a visit, I hastily clipped my son's hair and dashed for the atlas.

XIII

FULFILLMENT

With some misgivings I prepared for my trip to Pickway, Ontario. My apprehension sprang from conditions at home, rather than from expectations about the journey. My mind overflowed with anticipation concerning it, and I was eager to be off.

My fears grew out of the move we were making. For various reasons which I won't go into, Susie and I had sold our Rockydale home and had nearly completed the building of a small log dwelling near Hamburg. Much packing and sorting of clothing needed to be done. I didn't want my wife to do a man's work in lifting and lugging boxes and crates. However, Susie promised faithfully not to overdo in the packing.

Although our home was built of logs, its construction differed somewhat from its Northland cousins. Instead of being installed horizontally as most logs were in northern cabins, ours stood upright. Even if the house were small, it was home, and it reminded us continually of the Northland. As if we needed a reminder! And as usual, its construction left us with a mortgage.

I confess I could hardly wait for the meetings at Pickway to close. I felt that I must visit Royal and Margaret Fretz, although sixty miles lay between us, and although, as usual, I was eager to get back to Susie and the children. Therefore, following the close of services at Pickway, I lost no time in taking a train to Ducksbill.

"Guess what has happened since I saw you last, Brother!" Royal beamed after greeting me like a long lost brother. The light of heaven shone from his face. How my heart rejoiced. Margaret's expression reflected that same joy.

"What did, Brother?" I asked, taking a chair in their comfortable living room.

"We're going to move to Marshy Lake to live," Royal announced exuberantly. "It's all arranged."

"That's wonderful!" I cried. "Tell me, Roy. How did it all happen?"

Royal turned to Margaret. "Let's see, Margaret. Where shall I begin?"

Margaret's attractive face crinkled in a smile. "It really began with Bible school, Roy," she pondered. "We had planned to go for two weeks, you know, but . . . "

"Yes," Royal nodded, "but Brother Martz asked us if we could give two months instead. That rocked me." Royal grinned wryly. "I didn't see how I could possibly get away for eight weeks." Roy paused, remembering.

"But you did," I prompted.

"Yes," Royal replied happily. "The Lord had everything worked out. At that time our baby shoes were going exclusively to Eaton's and several other chain stores. I checked our supply, and we had enough on hand for two months' demand. We left with confidence to teach Bible school at Red Lake."

"The Lord does work things out when we allow Him to, doesn't He?" I asked, recalling vividly my own experience with this man.

"Yes, He certainly does!" Royal affirmed. He continued, "The conviction developed and grew in my heart, as we lived among the people, that this was where the Lord wanted us. I spoke to Margaret of this, but she wasn't so sure."

My glance went to Margaret. "I don't quite know why I hesitated, Brother Kenneth," she explained. "I think perhaps it may be more difficult for a woman to pull up roots and settle in an entirely different environment. That probably was part of the reason, and I really wasn't thoroughly convinced of the Lord's call in the matter."

"For awhile," Roy went on, "we didn't say much about it. Although it remained constantly in our minds, we avoided speaking of it. I did pray continually about it and asked the Lord to show Margaret His will." He smiled at his wife. "I knew we'd have to be united in this venture if it were to succeed."

"Well," I quipped, "you must have been convinced, Margaret. What happened?"

Margaret's grey eyes twinkled. "I held out until I got home," she replied. "When I entered the kitchen of this house, something told me that I didn't belong here . . ."

"Her first words were, 'I'll never be happy here,' " Royal concluded. "Oh, I was so glad to hear that! We sent an application almost immediately to Red Lake and have been accepted."

"Praise the Lord!" I cried. My mind raced to other considerations. "Your shoe business. What of it?"

Royal smiled triumphantly. "That was the really hard part, Kenneth," he stated. "As you know, the business had been given me by an old gentleman, Jack Lotts, who isn't a Christian. He had started it, worked with it, and built it into a successful enterprise. If anything should happen to it, or if it should flop, it would be like losing a child to Jack." Roy sat forward in his chair, hands sagging loosely between his knees.

"I can understand how you felt about it," I assured Royal, thinking of the reaction of the old man. "He probably wouldn't understand," I reasoned, "and accuse you of ingratitude and many other things."

"That was the way I had it figured," Royal conceded.

"Well, what did happen, Brother?" I probed.

Royal laughed. "It wasn't funny then," he acknowledged, "but one day as I struggled with the issue of approaching Jack, our deacon stopped by the shop for a chat. I almost shouted with relief. 'Here comes spiritual help!' I thought, but all he talked about was himself. I felt quite let down."

"I should think so!" I sympathized.

"In a way," Roy mused, sitting back in his contour chair, "it could have been my own fault. If I would have steered the conversation toward spiritual channels . . . Well, that's past, anyway."

Royal's face creased with amusement. "Kenneth, do you know what Jack Lotts said when I finally got up the nerve to tell him?"

"I can't imagine," I replied, leaning forward with anticipation.

" 'I expected it,' he said. 'I can't understand it, but I expected it,' " Royal told me reverently.

Laughter danced in Royal's eyes. "You know, Brother, for the second time that day I almost felt let down. I had prepared myself mentally for anything, and when nothing happened, I felt it would have almost been a relief if the old gentleman had blown his top!"

"Royal!" Margaret rebuked with a gentle laugh.

"So," Royal added, "we have hired a manager who is working with me until we go north in early August. "We're hoping," Royal said, spreading his hands wide, "to go as self-supporting missionaries."

My heart thrilled to my brother's account of the Lord's direction in his life.

I returned home to find a stack of mail awaiting me.

In the heap of mail demanding my attention was the acceptance which had arrived from Michael's school application. That meant, I decided, that Susie and I would need to keep our part of that agreement firmly in mind. We would supply the clothing and other incidentals if our son paid his own tuition.

At the moment, the money to keep that commitment was nowhere in sight.

XIV

CURLY

I prayed about the matter of money for Michael's school needs as Susie, the children, and I worked together preparing to move to our new home. The day came when the last item found its place in a box; we loaded the crates on a brother's truck and deposited them in our new dwelling.

Our move to Hamburg meant a change of grocery stores. As I stopped at the meat counter in the new store, a stranger spoke to me. In the ensuing conversation, I discovered that Mac Dellinger was a Christian but that our ideas differed widely in some areas. To my chagrin, he insisted that my view of these controversial subjects was "unbiblical."

"Mr. Dellinger," I protested as the conversation dragged on, "I really must be going. I've an appointment with Joe Hoover for a haircut at 9 p.m., and it's past that time already." I extended a hand. "Good-bye. It's been good meeting you."

Mac retained my hand, saying, "Mr. Eagle, I'd like to visit in your home one evening and explain the way of God more perfectly to you in this area of doctrine. When would it be convenient for you?"

Now I happened to be satisfied with the "way of the Lord" as He had revealed it to me through His Word, and I wasn't anxious to have Mac Dellinger attempting to convince me otherwise. I thought fast. "I'm tied up with meetings for several weeks," I answered, "then I've promised to teach in a winter Bible school for six weeks in western Pennsylvania." I considered, trying to be sincerely regretful "I'm sorry, but I don't have any free evenings for quite some time."

Mac Dellinger smiled amiably. "Keep it in mind, Sir," he remonstrated. "You are missing so much in the Christian life by excluding this area of doctrine from your practice."

"I'll think about it," I promised, picking up my bag of groceries. Mentally I determined that I would think of ways to avoid another confrontation with Mac Dellinger, especially in the haven of my own home!

I forgot Mac in the rush of preparing for meetings and in the hours of study necessary for teaching at the Bible school.

As I traveled from place to place and state to state, preaching and teaching the Gospel, I spoke often of the financial need at Red Lake. The mission now had an opportunity to purchase a larger plane, a Cessna 180. It would carry three passengers in addition to the pilot. It would cost $22,500.

That sounded like a fortune to this hill native. But its purchase made sense to me. It would be more expensive to operate but would actually save money by reducing the number of flights necessary to transport people and supplies. In reducing the number of trips, the mission would also save time which could be used in other necessary work.

Remembering my last trip north and the rattletrap condition of the plane I had ridden in and my mental determination to help the Lord answer Mamie's prayer, I set out immediately to do just that. I spoke often of the worn-out planes and the need for the Cessna.

I rejoiced as funds for the plane accumulated. I do not mean to imply that my efforts alone produced those funds—not at all. The Lord used many people and methods to bring together the necessary $22,500. Offerings came in from Amish groups, Christian day schools, family groups, and widows who were interested in the work. At last Brother Jones informed me the purchase of the plane would soon be possible.

In addition, the conviction burned in my heart that somewhere among our membership there must be a trained, competent mechanic just waiting for the Lord to tap him on the shoulder and say, "Come, I need you at Red Lake."

I never cease to marvel at the Lord's timing. He schedules even minute details to serve His omnipotent purposes. The work of His hand appeared much in evidence when the family and I drove to an all-day song fest in the village of Atglen.

The offering that day was to go specifically toward the purchase of the Cessna. The committee in charge asked me to speak, informing the gathering of 2,500 persons of the need for the plane and how it would be used.

I described as vividly as I could the worn-out planes that rattled and creaked; the dials and gauges that didn't work; the bubblegum, adhesive tape, and coal tar repairs. In my sincere belief that these planes were on their last leg of usefulness, I insisted that those planes were wrecks, not worth the cost of repairing. In an unconscious attempt to prove my point, I mentioned the five forced landings of the previous summer. I also emphasized the saving the larger plane would be to the mission.

That day's collection pushed the plane purchase "over the hump." However, the thrilling event of that day occurred at the close of the service.

As I stood chatting with a friend, I noticed a tall, slender man standing off to one side. He seemed to be waiting for an opportunity to speak to me. As soon as I decently could, I terminated my conversation and approached him.

I confess, Curly Mast caught me by surprise.

"Look, Brother Eagle," he exploded, "you don't just repair airplanes with adhesive tape and bubblegum, then expect them to fly like new! It's no wonder your pilots had to force land those planes," Curly sputtered indignantly.

Dumbfounded, I searched for a reply. Curly continued, "Planes don't wear out like cars do, Brother Eagle. You *never* junk an airplane. If you're a good mechanic, you overhaul them and they'll fly for years. If they're beyond overhauling, you keep them for parts."

My mind began functioning again. "You're an airplane mechanic, Curly?"

"Yes." His blue eyes flashed. He looked at me accusingly. "Did they ever really fix the one I worked on, the Piper Cub that went down in the cornfield?"

"Which plane was that, Curly?" I asked, trying to place it in my mind.

"The one that Allen Martz's brothers sent up—a twin to the one that went down in the lake with him and Jimmie," Curly explained.

"Oh, that one!" I thought a moment. Allen had not mentioned any repair cost that I could recall for that particular plane. I told Curly that I knew of none.

"You see!" he shot back, "I made just enough repairs on it to fly it up there. It needed more work done, but the mission was in too big a rush to let me do it properly. They promised to have it done up there. That plane isn't worn out. If I could get my hands on it, I'd show you!"

Realization struck like the shock of cold water. Before me stood my airplane mechanic! But I must move carefully lest I scare him off.

"Well," I said cheerfully, "if that's the way you feel, Curly, you ought to go up there. You're just the man they need."

"You're kidding, Brother Eagle," Curly replied, incredulity written all over his face.

"No, I'm not, Curly. They do need you. The mission pays thousands of dollars for plane repairs because the planes have to be flown south to Baudette, Minnesota—dollars that could be, saved if the work could be done on the spot."

Curly understood that. However, he failed to see himself as the "man of the hour," the Lord's man to meet this particular need.

"Just how many qualified mechanics, besides yourself, do you know in the church, Curly?" I probed.

Curly stuttered. "One, or perhaps two."

"Don't you think the Lord is calling you?" I insisted. "Don't you see the need?"

"Yes," Curly acknowledged. "I see that someone is needed, but I don't think I'm the one to go."

Other people pressed in to speak to me, but I sensed in Curly unfinished business. If I allowed my mechanic to escape now, before he had committed himself, he might be lost to the mission for good. I gently pushed the crowd aside.

The Lord nudged my memory as William Jones caught my attention. William had just returned from Red Lake. He planned to present a slide lecture in Bucks County the next Sunday. It just might work!

I corralled Curly into meeting William. The two "clicked" immediately. Eventually Curly agreed to drive quite a distance to view the slides. Somehow I sensed the victory had been won, although the course of events leading Curly to Red Lake had only begun.

XV

BIBLE SCHOOL SEND-OFF

Susie and I struggled during those months of summer to save enough money to keep our promise to Michael. It seemed impossible, however, to collect even a small amount that could be set aside for school expenses. I felt like rebelling. Inwardly I shouted, "Lord, You promised! Why don't You do something?"

Nevertheless, good news from the Northland cheered me. Royal and Margaret Fretz now carried responsibility for the work at Marshy Lake. Joy bubbled over in the correspondence that came our way. We rejoiced with them.

In addition to Royal, the Lord appeared to be drawing Curly Mast into the net, step by step. William Jones reported progress on this front.

"Yes," he stated happily, "Curly and his family did come to the slide program. We've visited back and forth several times since. They are nibbling with the idea of going to Red Lake. I don't believe it will be long before the Lord sets the hook."

We stood inside the church door at Hamburg. William stepped outside; I followed. "Did Curly check out the new plane?" I asked.

"Yes," William answered. "He was really pleased with it." He paused, and went on, chuckling, "But the idea that a plane that cost $22,500 will be sent that far, used hard, and perhaps not kept in good repair, is almost too much for him. It really is eating him. I've invited them to the dedication of the plane next Sunday. Will you be there, Kenneth?"

"No," I replied. "I'm leaving for a series of meetings in West Virginia tomorrow. I'll be gone for ten days."

Recalling Curly's reaction to my Atglen speech, I could imagine how he reacted to the purchase of this plane. Curly felt about planes as many young men do about their cars; they rate as objects of special care and devotion.

William broke a thin twig from the oak under which we stood. "Did you receive the last newsletter from Red Lake yet?" he asked.

"No," I replied. "Why do you ask?"

"I was wondering if you knew about the children's home that is being considered?" William returned.

I gaped in surprise. "Why no, I didn't. Tell me about it."

"Well, it simply boils down to the fact that the provincial government has asked the mission to provide a home for needy and neglected children, whether white or Indian," my friend explained.

"You know, William," I mused, "I'm told that there are no orphans in the bush, but that where liquor is easily available, it's a different story."

"I guess conditions compare with those of many underdeveloped areas and city ghettoes," William surmised, having glimpsed the problem briefly during his visit.

"Yes," I acceded. "It isn't only the underdeveloped regions and city ghettoes, though. We find alcoholism and child neglect in our small villages and larger towns, too. In fact, I saw an article about it in our local paper just yesterday." I pondered, "I wonder if these aren't universal problems."

The matter of neglected children slipped from my mind as I drove home to Susie and the family. Just as I prepared to turn in our lane, a horn beeped behind me. I pulled aside and stopped.

"Kenneth!" Mac Dellinger greeted me. "How are you today?"

"Fine, Mac. And how are you?" I turned to the car where a lovely young lady surveyed us with interest. "Your wife?" I questioned.

"Not yet, Kenneth," Mac informed me. "This is Linda Falls, my fiancee. Linda, meet Kenneth Eagle."

We enjoyed a pleasant chat. I dreaded the moment experience had taught me to expect. When would I have a convenient time to sit down and study the Word with them so they could teach me "more perfectly," to use their terminology.

I decided to beat them to the punch. "Mac," I stated,

"I've been thinking. I'm leaving tomorrow for meetings in West Virginia. I'll be gone for ten days. Call me after I get back, and I'll set a date for you to come over."

Mac's face lit with surprise. He gripped my hand. "I'll do that, Kenneth," he assured me. I had no doubt but that he would indeed!

September arrived. Michael approached us about school supplies. "I'll need them soon, Dad," he warned.

"I know, Son," I responded, "but things haven't gone as we had hoped they would. We don't have the money for everything you'll need. I think we may be able to supply your most urgent needs, such as the clothing, but that is all."

Michael walked away with sagging shoulders. I could almost hear him cry, "But, Dad, you promised!" My heart ached for the lad. Susie and I turned to our Lord for help.

The next day's mail dropped a "bombshell" into our laps. A letter came from the school containing a list of absolute essentials Michael must bring: one large box, one rug, two large single sheets, two heavy single blankets, a bedspread, pillow cases, a laundry bag, one pair of shower slippers, and a set of book ends.

Michael presented the list to Susie and me. Despair gripped my heart. "I'm sorry, Son," I said sadly, "but we just don't have the money. We'll try to get your shoes and things of that kind, but I can't swing this list too."

Mac Dellinger's call did nothing to ease my mind that Friday evening. I decided to invite him over and get the troublesome business behind me. He jumped at the invitation, stating that Linda would be with him.

They appeared promptly at 7:30 p.m. carrying their Bibles. We seated ourselves comfortably in our living room, facing the large window which offered a wide view of Pennsylvania's rolling hills. "Now, we'll lead you into the deeper things of the Spirit," Mac declared, opening his Bible.

Frankly, I didn't know how to cope with this situation. I told the Lord about it. He answered in the most amazing way, and one which I failed to recognize at the time—the telephone rang!

I listened with one ear to Susie's voice as she spoke to our caller; and with the other I tried to follow Mac's line of reasoning. In a few minutes Susie returned.

"That was Lillian Wade, Kenneth," Susie told us. "She wants me to come over to pick up her mother's clothing. They are trying to clear things out before the sale tomorrow. I guess I ought to go."

"Of course, Dear. Go ahead," I encouraged. I explained the circumstances to our guests. Susie departed, and we settled down for a period of discussion. Or rather, Mac spoke, Linda nodded agreement, and I listened. Mac's line of thinking baffled me. It left me at a loss for rebuttal.

Two hours later Susie burst into the house, her face glowing and radiant.

"Kenneth!" she cried. "Praise the Lord! What do you think happened?"

"I've no idea, Susie. What did happen?" I asked wonderingly, sensing that something out of the ordinary had transpired.

"Bring this box in for me, and I'll tell you about it," Susie instructed joyously.

Mac aided me in lugging a large box into the house. We stood by as Susie began to remove things from it. As she worked, she talked.

"After giving me these things belonging to her deceased mother, Mrs. Wade turned to these other articles and said, 'Here are some odds and ends—pillow cases, sheets, book ends, and the like. Would you have any use for them?' Kenneth, I could have jumped up and down with joy, I was so excited."

I didn't doubt her. Her joy and happiness fairly bubbled even now. Mac and Linda looked on wonderingly.

"You see," I explained to our guests, "these are all things our son needs to go to Bible school in a few weeks. We had told him we would get them for him, but we couldn't because we didn't have the money. . . ."

Susie's eyes gleamed as she picked up her story. "I told Mrs. Wade that those were just what Michael needed to take along to school. She looked rather startled, then said, 'I have some other things I wonder if he could use.' She came back with this rug," and Susie held it up for our appraisal, "brand new, never been used, and this bedspread, blankets, and laundry bag. She dug out this big old box to put everything in, so we now have everything on Michael's list except the shower slippers! Isn't our God wonderful?"

"He is indeed!" I echoed, almost speechless, especially when I recalled my own rebellion and lack of faith in His providence.

"But that isn't all, Dear," Susie added jubilantly. "Just look at these."

I stared in awe as Susie held up shoes, almost new, a suit that had never been worn, shirts, and socks—all gifts from the Lord through Lillian Wade. Michael walked in, and the clothing proved to be a perfect fit. Why shouldn't it have been? After all, God always does everything well!

When our excitement abated somewhat, I explained more to Mac and Linda what our predicament had been. They had seen the Lord's solution for themselves.

Mac Dellinger shook his head in disbelief. "I've never seen it on this wise," he quoted humbly. "Do things like this happen to you often?"

I quietly told him of our commitment to the Lord's work and our agreement to trust the Lord where our physical welfare was concerned. I told him of various means the Lord had employed in supplying our needs, including my recent experience in Grand Forks, North Dakota. "It has been a wonderful adventure; don't you agree, Dear?"

"Yes," Susie acknowledged. "I wouldn't want to live any other way."

This led to a discussion of "unique" Mennonite doctrines and their basis in Scripture, including the woman's veiling commanded in I Corinthians 11. Mac and Linda readily accepted this, and they vowed on the spot to practice this Scriptural teaching.

When our guests left, Mac shook my hand feelingly. "We came here to teach you some things, but we have learned much in your home. We thank you."

Later Susie and I were invited to their wedding.

However, since it fell at a time when I had to be elsewhere, I could not attend. Susie related the outstanding part of the ceremony for me.

"Just before the ceremony while the couple were kneeling, a friend of the bride placed a veil upon the bride's head, as a symbol of her acceptance of her husband's headship. It was really impressive, Kenneth."

"I'm sure that symbol means something to them," I pondered.

"Yes," Susie assented. "It will probably mean more to them than to those of us who have lived with it from infancy and hardly know why we wear it," Susie mused.

"I'm afraid that is true," I nodded.

Susie added, "Linda has continued to wear the veil, in spite of the fact that their church does not teach it."

How I rejoiced as I considered God's overruling hand in the matter of Mac Dellinger!

The Lord continued His operation upon the resistance of Curly Mast, but I didn't learn the details of that surgery until later.

XVI

VISION CAPTURED

"This is not mission work." I read the statement in a letter from Royal Fretz. It jarred me completely. My young friend in the Northland had asked the opinion of an elderly, seasoned missionary about the work being conducted by Northern Light Gospel Mission. That astonishing assessment had been his reply.

I hastened to read further. The older man, Royal continued, had gone on to explain that mission work to him consists of hardship, living very simply, going without necessities, and doing things by hand. I could hear Royal chuckle as he added that his elderly friend would have found it impossible to fit into their program of airplanes, two-way radio, swamp buggies, sawmills, and many other innovations. To him, mission work consisted of entirely different elements.

By this time my mind rocked. We believed we had followed the Lord's leading in each new venture. But we also valued the ideas of others, especially those of veteran missionaries whom the Lord had blessed. I hurried to read further.

"Brother Smith then quoted part of Joel 2:28," Royal wrote, " ' . . . your old men shall dream dreams, your young men shall see visions.' He went on to say that he lives in the dreams of the past. We younger men must carry the vision for the present; without it we perish." I breathed a sigh of relief, just as I'm sure Royal must have done.

I read more. "My newest vision is so preposterous, Kenneth, that I wonder if I'm going off half-cocked. I was over at Cains Bay the other day. Several men were gathered in one of the homes. We were discussing how to make a better living for local families. You know, Kenneth, in our affluence, we don't realize what a struggle it is to make ends meet here in the bush. Did you know that gasoline is $1.55 a gallon here, and flour $18 per 100 pounds? The average Indian earns about

$1,000 per year from trapping and fishing."

What was Royal leading up to? Some plan simmered in his mind, I was positive.

"My interest in the problem stems from the fact that I live here, too. Also, I have learned that telling others that 'Jesus cares' is of little value unless I demonstrate it by doing something positive myself."

"As I see it," Roy stated, "our storehouses are full and overflowing. I'm not referring to our canned goods and other supplies of food, but to our store of knowledge. And with our wide range of knowledge comes responsibility to share that knowledge with our fellowmen."

Susie smiled. "That is true," she acknowledged. "I wonder what Royal is proposing."

I grinned in return. "We'll get to it presently."

"We discussed the feasibility of gardens—growing potatoes, perhaps," Roy continued. "While we agreed that the idea had possibilities, we were concerned about how the land could be cleared. You know the type of land cover we have here, Kenneth, and we have no horses or equipment to work with."

My mind raced. How did men in our area go about such work? Bulldozers? Tractors? Grubbing hoes?

"I asked Manuel Moose," Royal went on, "if we could get a tractor in to Marshy Lake. This would mean crossing an area of 150 miles of bush, lakes, and muskeg. As you are aware, Kenneth, there are no roads. The trip would have to be made in the dead of winter. Manuel promised if I could find a tractor and get it in as far as Todd's Lake, 30 miles from Marshy Lake, he would personally meet me there for the rest of the trip in."

Susie and I looked at each other. Whether Royal's plan was half-cocked or not, we didn't know. But we could, and did, pray about it. We told the Lord that if this was His will, we were trusting Him to supply either the tractor or the money to purchase one. We left it in His hands.

Mentally I added that tractor to Mr. Smith's list of modern day missionary equipment that did not "fit in."

My friend, William Jones, dropped in that same day.

I told him of Royal's plan, and William promptly handed me a ten-dollar bill.

"To start the tractor rolling," he smiled.

"Thank you, and God bless you, Brother."

"I've brought good news for you, Kenneth," he said.

"Oh? What is it?" I asked. "Has Curly decided to go to Red Lake?"

"You take the wind right out of my sails," William sighed, settling back in his chair.

"How did it happen? How soon is he going?" I asked eagerly.

"Well, you know he and his family attended the dedication for the Cessna, don't you?" William remarked.

"I knew they had planned to."

"They came," William confirmed. "There were several quartet numbers sung by myself and three other men. Curly told me later that it seemed as if those songs were meant just for him. And the thought of sending that plane up there and knowing that it would not be kept in top condition, was too much for him. He and Allen are corresponding about the matter now and seeking to find the Lord's will for both of them."

"Praise the Lord!" I cried. Susie echoed my joy.

"There are some hang-ups," William warned.

"Oh?"

Curly has no facilities at Red Lake in which to work and not enough funds to purchase any," William elaborated. "They are considering the possibility of building a hangar with mission funds. In return, Curly will do mission repairs without charge, while doing other work or plane repair jobs for his support." William pondered the scheme as he stood at our front window. I studied his broad back.

"With the amount of flying done in the area, it sounds as if it might be a good plan," I conjectured. "The closest repair service is Baudette, Minnesota."

William turned to face us. "Everyone concerned is praying about this. It will take some time to get through all the red tape and get the building put up . . . Meanwhile, Curly will need a place to work."

"I'm sure something will turn up," I responded

glibly, never suspecting how wrong I would prove to be on that point.

After all, I reasoned, the Lord had called Curly to this place of service and had moved him to answer that call. Surely the mission would do their part in providing a place in which he could work. However, I could not foresee the magnitude of Curly's physical ordeal before the mission-built hangar became a reality.

News also of Clayton Drake's progress seeped through to me from various sources. Allen Martz made a trip south, speaking in a number of churches. He spent several days with us. I used the opportunity to ask about my young friend.

"Clayton is an excellent teacher," Allen informed me. "He has developed his own methods. As you are aware, Kenneth, the children speak only their tribal dialect when they come to school, so they are also learning a new language along with the other skills."

"How does one go about teaching a new language?" I asked.

"Well, Clayton presents a picture, perhaps of a dog," Allen explained. "He identifies it as a dog. Then he places the word 'dog' beside the picture of the dog. He has the pupils to draw a dog and label it. He may have the children make up a story about a dog. He uses word cards, the blackboard, and many other devices to help fix the word in their minds."

I whistled. "I see now why Jimmie says he is up until 1 a.m. at times preparing the next day's school work," I remarked.

Allen smiled quietly. "We are really pleased with the way the children are learning."

"Good, good!" I rejoiced.

"There has been another development," Allen informed me.

"Oh?"

"Brother Sam and Brother Moses have asked us to conduct a boarding school for their children. You know, when the parents are out on the trap lines, the children may miss several months of school. If we had a place to house the children . . . "

"I see," I murmured.

Allen also relayed another piece of news. An election would determine who would operate the day school at Bear River. If the people chose to have the province supply a teacher, Clayton Drake would be out of a job. I sensed a momentary forboding, then forgot the matter.

Somehow, my mind failed to connect these developments with Mamie's prayer for a school. I marveled later at my blindness!

XVII

TRACTOR TREK—WEEK ONE

"Praise the Lord, Susie!" I exclaimed as I read a letter from Royal Fretz. "A Toronto businessman is delivering the tractor free from that point to Red Lake on his truck. That is 1300 miles," I told Susie. "Now all they have to do is take it the remaining 150 miles overland from Red Lake to Marshy Lake."

Some changes had been made before bringing the tractor north, Royal stated. Half tracks had replaced the rear wheels. Skis were installed on the front end. A platform at the rear served as storage area for gasoline and other necessities, including the food box.

The groundwork for the journey had been meticulously carried out by Royal and Curly Mast, who had moved north some time before with his family. The two men flew over the route several times, studying the terrain: lakes, river channels, muskeg, rock ledges, and anything else that might affect the journey.

We knew that Royal and Curly planned to start in with the tractor the first Monday in December. We determined to pray much for their success and safety.

Sometime later I received an account of that experience from Royal.* Parts of it follow:

"What a sight to behold! One new Massey-Ferguson 35 all painted and new, standing on the ice at Red Lake, only approximately 150 miles through frozen forest from its future home. At that time we rejoiced greatly at the prospects, not realizing all the heartaches that we would face in taking it into Marshy Lake.

"The mission plane took me out to Red Lake on a weekend so we could get an early start on Monday morning. The rear platform of the tractor stood loaded with three ten-gallon drums of gasoline, a two-way radio, tools, a box of grub, and other items one anticipated as needs on such a trip.

"It was still dark when Curly and I left the mission for points north. There were no farewells, partly because it was too early in the morning, and partly because people generally felt we wouldn't get too far anyway!

"There are several hazards to winter travel that I ought to explain. Experience is a good thing; this we both lacked. I have learned since that few experiences parallel. So much depends on snow conditions and other factors. The only safe rule to follow is common sense.

"Frequent danger is thin ice. Conditions vary on the same lake. This may be caused by currents; strong currents erode the ice, and what was safe last week may not be safe today. A large snowfall can easily cause six inches of good ice to submerge. This causes the water to rise above the ice and saturate the snow, creating slush. The slush then freezes but it makes poor ice to travel over. There were very few times that the tractor did not break through the slush ice we traveled across.

"Muskeg presents another problem. As you know, Kenneth, (Only at that time, I didn't! I learned later, however!) muskeg is a bottomless bog. The only way to travel over it is when the surface is frozen. If a muskeg is covered with snow before the surface freezes, it will not freeze. Traveling over it is almost as impossible as it would be without the snow.

"Another hazard to deal with is the weather. Bitter cold can be a silent killer. At 55 degrees below zero, you can pour water out of a glass, and it will freeze before it hits the ground."

I whistled in astonishment. Susie looked at me questioningly. "You can have this page in a minute, Dear," I promised.

"Added to the other perils is the constant danger of getting lost. The forests are a network of trails made by trappers. These follow from one lake into the next. We anticipated using an old trail that followed the lowlands into Marshy Lake."

I paused in my reading to say to Susie, "I'm glad I didn't realize how perilous this undertaking was before those men started out!"

"I know," Susie agreed. She pondered the dangers Royal had named. "You know, Kenneth," she added, "I really have to admire Margaret Fretz. I don't know if I could have agreed to let *you* start out on such a risky venture or not!"

I grinned teasingly at Susie and turned back to Royal's report.

"By noon of the first day," Roy continued, "we had traveled the length of Red Lake and entered our first portage. We soon learned that this was altogether different than lake travel. The snow was four feet deep, which completely covered small trees and brush.

"We worked over an hour just getting the rig off the lake and onto land. We were almost disheartened when we thought of the many more portages ahead of us. When we finally got going, we had to use second gear, low range. This was slower than the speed of walking, but at least we were moving!

"We also discovered, Kenneth, that one of us had to sit on the hood of the tractor to keep it from rearing up at the front. Otherwise the driver might lose control, and we would find ourselves heading up some stately pine! Can't you picture that?"

I could indeed! I chuckled in spite of myself.

"That first afternoon brought disappointment. Everything seemed to be going so well. Both Curly and I were happy and felt we were well on the way. We didn't realize we were in a flooded area of the bush—flooding caused by an energetic colony of beavers. Without realizing it, we headed straight for the snow-covered dam. The dam broke away, and the next instant all of the tractor except the engine and front wheels went under."

Susie, who was now reading over my shoulder, gasped. I echoed her reaction.

"Curly and I surveyed the situation," we read. "We decided to call Red Lake by radio and have them drop us a hand winch. This was done. An hour later the Cessna 180 dropped the necessary equipment on an adjacent lake. Six hours later we successfully winched the tractor out of the mud and water onto a log platform we had built so that the ice would carry the weight. We were soon off the danger zone and heading north."

"I don't understand, Kenneth . . . " Susie puzzled.

"I can't explain it, Susie," I interrupted. To be

truthful, I was too anxious to read on to try to show Susie how the recovery had been accomplished!

"Due to the episode at the dam," Royal wrote, "our feet had become wet. While working on the tractor this didn't bother us too much. However, when we left the portage and drove out onto Trillium Lake, we faced into a blizzard. A stiff northwesterly blew, dropping temperatures down to 40 degrees below. Our clothing froze in minutes; we soon realized we were in danger of freezing our feet."

Susie and I shared a concerned gasp and hastened on.

"It would have been folly to try to remedy the problem on the open lake. Our only hope lay in reaching a tourist camp at the northern end of Trillium Lake. Visibility was at times nil, due to the storm. We feared we might get lost. This could happen easily on a lake fifteen miles long. Several times during the night we got stuck in a snowdrift, but because of the shoveling and God's mercy, we did not freeze our feet. By 5 a.m. Tuesday, we reached the tourist camp."

I breathed a sigh of relief and said, "Praise the Lord!"

Royal continued, "The code of the North is understood by everyone. Whenever you leave your home or camp, you always have dry kindling and firewood next to the heater. By chance someone may come by and need a fire immediately; it could mean the difference between life and death. This was how we found the camp. In minutes we had a fire, some hot food, and were ready to sleep.

"The next few days were uneventful. It was slow going; we soon realized it would take much longer to reach Marshy Lake than we had anticipated. Every night we built a fire to try to dry our clothing, and in a few hours we were quite damp. At 60 degrees below it proved next to impossible to dry our garments. The extreme cold and heat caused condensation, so while one side dried, the other side was getting damp.

"Our first layover was to be at Moonsoonie, 55 air miles north of Red Lake. Joe Brooks and his wife are there you remember, Kenneth. We had hoped to reach this station by the middle of the first week, but it appeared we might not make it by the end of that week.

"We arrived at Diamond Lake, one spot where Curly and I had expected problems when charting our route. Trappers who know the country advised us to go around it, rather than over it. However, there were high rocks to the right, and muskeg to the left. This left no choice but the muskeg. We soon learned we were in the worst bog we had yet encountered. By sunset we were immobile. In fact, it appalled us to realize that our machine was sinking in the muskeg!"

A low groan escaped my lips and Susie gulped. We had to find out how the men had saved the tractor. We quickly read on.

"After looking to God for wisdom, we felt our only hope would be to shovel the snow away from around the vehicle. This caused the subzero temperatures to freeze the surface so quickly that the tractor would sink no further. After doing this, we were so pleased with the result that we cleared a roadway back out to the end of Diamond Lake. It was something to behold as the frozen shell broke away from the half tracks but the momentum of the machine kept it on top.

"Kenneth, there were many altars erected along the way. Neither time nor paper would allow me to mention the many times we called on God. Every time we stalled in a windfall, prayer was made. There were literally hundreds of places when it looked as though we would have to spend much time, but God made a way. His Name was constantly on our lips.

"By Friday night we were only twelve miles from Moonsoonie. The Grey River flows through this area. When one thinks of our northern rivers, we don't think of them as waterways that reach from bank to bank, following a clear-cut course. Our rivers also take in lake areas, and the stream or current can follow a given course through a maze of waterways. This was the case on this Friday night. We had lost the trail and feared to drive farther lest we get on poor ice.

"Both of us had come close to exhaustion due to the cold and lack of sleep. It was hard to believe that we were only twelve miles from friends and a warm bed, yet not know which way to go. Curly draped himself over the steering wheel of the tractor, trying to absorb as much warmth as possible. I donned a pair of snowshoes and set out to try to find the trail. After walking through the bush for hours without success, I really wondered if it was worth all the effort.

"My tears froze to my cheeks; the sweat from my forehead formed icicles on my eyebrows. I constantly picked the ice off my lashes so my eyes would not paste shut. I looked up into the clear night sky to seek my Father's face and beg Him to show us where to find the trail."

I confess that tears of sympathy formed in my own eyes as I read of the trials of my brother. I knew God had heard his plea. I must know how He had answered it. I hastily returned to Roy's report of that incident.

"As I stood there," he wrote, "I saw the Northern Lights play their silent sonata as those mysterious fingers of light seemed to touch the very treetops. Other than the distant purr of the tractor, all was still—so still that the frost crystals seemed to crackle as they glittered in the moonlight.

"Every place around us looked impassable. Only one area seemed hopeful. It bordered a creek. Poplar trees three inches or more in diameter covered the area. I felt that God was directing us to this spot along the creek. The poplars snapped off like match sticks as we headed the tractor along this route. Severe cold makes the wood brittle; a small amount of pressure will break a tree. After mushing along the river for one mile, we found the trail.

"When we broke out of the last portage, my eyes feasted on the flicker of lights that came from Indian homes in the settlement of Moonsoonie. I thanked God that here we would find food, warm beds, and Christian fellowship. Almost more dead than alive, we staggered into Moonsoonie.

"Both of us were flown home to our families on Saturday. On Monday morning we were back, ready for another week of travel.

"From Moonsoonie to Bear River is only twenty-five miles by air, but our route would be nearly double that.

We expected to make good time on this leg of the trip because it was the shortest part, and the best as far as the contour of the land was concerned."

They deserve some good luck once, I thought to myself. Little did I dream that three more weeks of travel lay between the men and their destination!

*This account was taken from a booklet "The Northern Light Our Lamp" published by Northern Light Gospel Mission. It has been edited briefly.

XVIII

TRACTOR TREK (PART TWO)

"All had gone well until we reached the river that connected Foggy Lake and a neighboring body of water," Roy continued in his report of their efforts to get the Massey-Ferguson tractor overland to Marshy Lake.

"We edged the tractor out of the portage onto the arm of Foggy at 10 p.m. on Monday. We took the needle bar, a device for checking the thickness of the ice, and walked along our proposed route and measured the ice depth. If there was any other way, we decided, we would avoid this one! Our tests showed that the ice at most places was only a few inches thick. The only good thing about the situation was that the water beneath the ice was only five feet deep!

"We knew we had to take the risk. Everything seemed to go well for a quarter of a mile. The tractor shuddered, along with the sound of breaking ice. Moments later we had again dropped the back half of the machine in the water. We were fortunate because again the engine was still above the surface and the carry-all platform had prevented the back from going in deeper than the seat.

"After hours of constructing a log platform to keep it from sinking deeper and several fruitless attempts to raise the tractor onto the ice, we gave up. That night Curly couldn't rest. He had come to the place where physically he was at the end of his part in the trip.

"Morning found us very discouraged. We were too far from a tree to use the tackle. The situation called for another huddle with the Heavenly Father for direction.

"At 9 a.m. we heard the drone of a plane. After you live by flying, you become familiar with the many types of planes and can distinguish the sound of individual crafts. At a great distance we recognized this plane as a

Cessna 180. Dared we hope it to be the trader from my station? Margaret had asked him to check on us as he made his routine flights. How glad we were when he pulled full flaps and came in!

"Curly climbed aboard without knowing that a full week in the hospital lay ahead of him in recuperating from this adventure."

"That's too bad, Susie!" I cried.

"Yes," Susie acknowledged, "but I have to think of the courage and determination of those men for sticking with it when the going got rough." We hastened to finish Roy's account.

"Kenneth, if you have never been alone, 50 air miles from the nearest town, in weather 50 degrees below zero, and with a tractor stuck in the lake, and with it your duty to get it out, you would find it difficult to imagine what enters the mind. We say that man's extremity is God's opportunity. This makes wonderful pulpit material in an oil-heated cathedral, but out in the bush under adverse circumstances, it doesn't make quite the same theological sense!

"Nevertheless, God has over and over again glorified Himself when we rely fully upon Him. This happened at Foggy Lake. Looking back, I see the hand of God.

"Kenneth, after the plane left that morning I simply told God how things were and that we needed to get the tractor out of that hole. I don't recall all of the incident, but I do remember chaining several logs together, and somehow winching the rig out of the water. It was almost unbelievable that alone, before my new helper arrived, I had the tractor out and again headed north."

"Praise the Lord!" Susie and I breathed in unison.

"While much of the trip was sobering, we also had times of lighter veins," Roy continued. Susie and I were ready for something cheering, so we hurried to discover what Royal could possibly have found laughable about such a venture.

He surprised us. "I shall refrain from mentioning names," we read, "since I don't wish to embarrass anyone. The young man flown in to replace Curly was fresh from his father's farm in Pennsylvania. I found him to be a fine Christian man, but green to the bush.

Soon after his arrival he informed me that he would like to accompany me all the way to Marshy Lake. He was fresh, and had dry clothing, and was enjoying the thrill of a new experience. I said little, because I felt that after the sun went down and the night noises were heard, perhaps the hearth might call a little stronger than he realized.

"We crossed the arm of Foggy Lake and headed into a fifteen-mile portage. After several hours it became apparent that we had gotten off the trail and were lost. I tramped around trying to find it, without success. Finally it became obvious that the only thing to do was make camp and wait until morning.

"My farmer friend watched eagerly as I shoveled snow from the moss. Then I pulled the tarp from the rig and spread it on the moss as a bed. He then spoke up and asked where we would sleep. I informed him that I was making our bed. I suppose he could tolerate the bed, but when I handed him a can of frozen pork and beans, he kindly told me I was carrying things a mite too far. Someone had told him that one could get food poisoning eating directly out of tins, and frozen in the bargain. I felt very selfish as I chipped the beans out of my tin, enjoying every morsel. I tried to encourage him to eat, too. After our devotions that night, he stated that he had spoken too hastily; he had changed his mind about going farther than Bear River.

"The next morning brought with its golden glory new encouragement. We found the trail and were soon heading toward Bear River.

"With the route from Bear River to Red Lake behind us, we got the feeling that we were almost home. The truth is that we were only slightly more than halfway. The novelty of bush travel had worn off, and we solemnly faced the facts. North of Clancy Lake is a large muskeg, and it lay on our direct route. The area is so unfriendly that even the wild animals avoid it. Trappers of the Clancy Lake country told us the big muskeg had not frozen over. They feared it to be impassable.

"My traveling companion from Bear River was to be a veteran, a man of the Grey River people. I was delighted to have him as my associate, being confident that he knew the dangers ahead and was capable of forewarning me if the need arose.

"I have great respect for these people of the forest. They are wise to the way of life here in the bush country. We had only one problem—communication. My friend spoke no English, and I could not speak Cree, his native tongue.

"In a short time I was able to determine the meaning of some of the words and signs my guide used," Royal went on. "I'd purposed in my heart that as long as he stayed on the hood, I would not desert my machine. Many times the wheels broke through the slush ice, and I was never sure if the ice beneath would carry the stress. At such times I was torn betwixt two decisions, whether to jump or stay put. So when the slush ice gave way, I watched the expression of my buddy on the hood. As long as he had a confident expression, I was determined to stay with my ship!

"We arrived at Clancy in record time. Could it be that the muskeg wouldn't be as bad as we had anticipated? We would have to wait and see.

"A heavy growth of spruce and pine borders the muskeg. As we weaseled our way out of this, for the first time in my life I saw this area from the ground. It was a great sea of silent snow. Large mounds covered the area, formed by the plant life and foliage that grew there. Because of the rocky hills surrounding the place, little drifting occurred.

"This muskeg had earned its respect because it had many times defied man. As I stood and looked out over that great expanse, I knew for certain that unless God undertook for us, we would have to write the epitaph for the Massey-Ferguson."

They got there, I know, I thought to myself. How did they do it? I must find out.

Roy continued. "Kenneth, I reasoned, 'Would God want us to tell those who gave of their means to make this venture a success that their investment now lies buried in a muskeg north of Clancy Lake?' No, I decided, this couldn't be His will. I removed my parka hood and laid hands on that tractor and asked my God to bless it.

"My faith was sorely tried only minutes later. I had gone a short distance when the tractor trembled as though it had an attack of the palsy. It settled in the mire, to stay there for several days. Hours of shoveling, carrying poles, and every effort imaginable followed. It seemed futile; all our work failed to get us moving again.

"If only I would have had someone to pray with! Before, Curly had been with me, and we could stand at Bethel together. Now, spiritually, I was alone. It seemed that my hope of getting the tractor in had received its death blow; this predicament was its death throe. Soon everything would be over, and we could go home and write it all down under the section marked 'Experience.'

"To make matters worse, a blizzard moved in, and the weather became what we call 'zero, zero.' Nights were spent in silent despair and solitude. The very remoteness of our location seemed to scream, 'Defeat! Defeat!' I lay for hours listening to the wind moaning through the pines, wondering what the message was—if it could be interpreted. Yet, I dare not believe that God was not there!

"How wonderful it was to see blue sky after several days of wind and snow! And how much more wonderful to hear the approach of the first plane after the storm. We had the understanding that if we did not gesture to the pilot, all was well. If we waved our arms, the pilot would attempt to land nearby and assist us. I had to restrain myself from giving Jimmie Byler a hero's welcome while he circled us with his little J-3. There was really nothing he could do. It was up to us to work out a plan to get out of the muskeg.

"But, oh! how graceful that little plane looked up there! I almost wished the Massey-Ferguson people made flying machines rather than tractors. It reminded me of Isaiah 40:31. So many of us get bogged down in the muskeg of life, like the tractor, when we should be soaring above, like that little J-3."

"That's an apt comparison, Susie," I remarked. But my wife hadn't stopped reading to listen to me talk. Oh,

I realized suddenly. The tractor was still in the muskeg! But Roy, I discovered, didn't return to the tractor immediately in his narrative.

"When Jimmie's wife Lydia heard that Jimmie was checking on us, she thought it would be nice to give us fellows a touch of home. So when Jimmie banked the Cub, he dropped a bag of sandwiches. Home-baked bread with sloppy joe filling, made from moose meat! Oh, how delicious and scrumptious! I was convinced beyond doubt that a moose had never died for a more noble cause!

"Nothing had changed," Susie and I read, "where the tractor was concerned. The bog still held it; we had found no way of freeing it. I know of only one way to explain what happened that cold, bright morning in the muskeg above Clancy Lake.

"Just how many people were praying for us, we'll never know. I do know that all the mission personnel were constantly lifting us to the throne. Several churches in eastern Ontario were interceding for us. This is the only explanation I can offer for what happened that morning.

"As I faced our situation, I had a strong compulsion to get on the tractor and drive it. This I did, and to my utter astonishment we began to move. I was so startled that I dared not stop to pick up our equipment which lay scattered around from our fruitless efforts during the past few days.

"It was certainly beyond the natural, Kenneth. As I looked to my right and to my left, the trees literally vibrated. The tops shook as far away as several hundred feet, due to the vibration of the tractor and the type of bog we were in. It seemed as though a giant hand pushed us through the length of the muskeg. We didn't stop once until we were out on high ground."

Susie and I breathed a prayer of thanksgiving and praise.

"The third week had passed since Curly and I had left Red Lake. We arrived now at Todd's Lake, and my guide was in unfamiliar country. Here another friend, Manuel Moose, who was like a grandfather to me, was to meet us.

"The Todd's Lake region and north is a network of water, where a good guide is essential. At several places it is very important whether you are fifty feet from the right shore or the left. In some places our safety depended upon which way we passed an island. Because of God's grace and the good judgement of Manuel, we finally arrived at Marshy Lake, almost five weeks after leaving Red Lake.

"Kenneth, I'll never forget the excitement our arrival created. For the first time the people of Marshy Lake saw a tractor. As far as the village is concerned, Gemini 5 didn't create as much of a stir as that tractor did! It received its official name that Friday, Wabus Otaban, the first word meaning rabbit, the second meaning vehicle. The vehicle received this name because the tractor had large 'legs' in the back, smaller ones in the front."

Royal's report now assumed a more personal touch. "I know you are wondering if we have seen any tangible results from this effort. One of the most encouraging remarks overheard was by a young man, who said, 'Now I really believe this white man loves us.'

"There are bound to be those who believe this whole venture a mistake. However, I would rather launch out for God and find I have made a mistake, than do nothing at all for fear of making a mistake. God can glorify Himself through our errors, but He cannot glorify Himself if we do nothing."

How true! I mused. I hadn't thought of it in that way before.

"Satan is trying hard to discourage us," Royal added, turning to other matters. "We are told that there will never be a Christian here. Perhaps the person of greatest influence is Gitchie Martha. Please pray for her, Kenneth. Remember that two men praying the same prayer anywhere on earth will raise a commotion in heaven. If she were converted, probably many others would come too. Shall we claim our Lord's promise in Matthew 18:19 and unite in praying for her, Brother?"

He added a sobering thought, "Remember, too, that we go only as far in the Christian life as we go on our knees."

The last item on Royal's communication concerned his former shoe manufacturing business. "The last report shows the business again in the red. Doesn't the Lord *want* us to be self-supporting missionaries?"

Doesn't He indeed?

XIX

ON THE BATTLE FRONT

It seems that when people are on fire for the Lord and souls are being saved, Satan also gets busy. The Northland was no exception.

Curly Mast had found no place suitable for use as an airplane repair shop. Consequently, he worked outdoors far into the winter, in all kinds of weather, until the hangar was ready for use.

"Curly finds it very discouraging," Allen Martz told me via the mail routes. "He is pretty much on the fence. He gets plenty of work but has had trouble collecting his money. Also he has had trouble in finding enough qualified help to keep up with the work. We do hope conditions will improve and he will decide to stay." He added, "I don't know what we would do without him."

"I'll write to him and try to encourage him," I told Susie.

In communicating with Curly, I discovered that Allen had not understated Curly's difficulties. However, Curly agreed to trust the Lord and hang on for awhile longer. That settled that conflict for the time being.

An item from the newsletter chilled me as I thought of our mission families. This one concerned the Joe Brooks family, but I thought of Royal and Margaret and their small sons as I read it.

"Listen to this, Susie," I said. I began reading: "An old lady on the reserve who has a reputation for this kind of thing and carries a grudge against the Gospel, tried to put a curse on our baby. Babies are easy victims. The people believe that if the curse is successful, the baby dies, and the remainder of his life is added to the life of the one who cursed him. Expectant mothers are common victims because two lives are gained."

Susie shuddered. "Kenneth, do you . . ." the sentence hung, unfinished.

I knew what Susie meant. "Susie, Satan has far greater power than most of us can imagine or give him credit for. I'm sure this account would not appear here had it not actually happened. Shall I finish reading it?"

"Yes, Dear. Please do."

"If the curse does not work," I continued, "it will return to the family or near relative of the one who put the curse. That is what happened in our case. The Lord protected us because we prayed. I wish people at home would pray, too."

The last sentence of that letter wrung our hearts. "Sometimes we almost feel like giving up because of the great strength of the evil power against us."

Cause for concern plagued us from another area. The mail brought a letter from Clayton Drake. The election had been held at Bear River and the mission had lost; they no longer had the privilege of conducting the day school there. Since he no longer held a teaching position, Clayton stated that he and his wife had packed and were going back to Pennsylvania.

"Susie! This can't be!" I protested. "Surely God didn't go to all that trouble to show Clayton His will, just to end his usefulness this suddenly!"

"I see," Susie replied thoughtfully.

"What do you see, Susie?" I asked, partly in seriousness.

"I'm not sure, Kenneth," my wife returned. "It just seems to me that the Lord must have a finger in this entire situation somewhere. Let's just turn it over to Him, shall we?"

In turning Clayton and his future over to God, we also found it necessary to commit Royal and his family, and all the other workers, over to the Heavenly Father. There had been no crack in the hard shell surrounding Gitchie Martha. Did the same danger surround the Fretz children which had threatened those of Joe Brooks? Only the Lord knew, and only He could protect them. And would the Spirit be able to penetrate the hard heart of this elderly woman? Again, only our Heavenly Father knew.

Where will it all end? The Lord had moved mightily in answering our cry for workers in the Northland. The enemy had come out full force to oppose them. How would the battle go?

What of Gitchie Martha? We had been praying earnestly for her. Would she come to know the Lord? And if she did, would her influence lead others to accept Him too, as we hoped it would?

The Lord had raised up Lee James as a voice for Himself. Would there be others? What of Jim and Moses? I had not met these brethren, but they demonstrated real qualities of leadership. Were they perhaps part of the answer?

Had Clayton Drake completed his work in the North? Could God use Wabus Otaban as a tool to further His kingdom, or had this investment been futile? Would Curly stay or give up?

Surely the Lord, who knows all about spiritual battle, knew the answers to these questions. We knew He could be trusted for the unfolding future.

Christian Light Publications, Inc., is a nonprofit conservative Mennonite publishing company providing Christ-centered, Biblical literature in a variety of forms including Gospel tracts, books, Sunday school materials, summer Bible school materials, and a full curriculum for Christian day schools and homeschools.

For more information at no obligation or for spiritual help, please write to us at:

Christian Light Publications, Inc.
P. O. Box 1212
Harrisonburg, VA 22801-1212